FIELD ATHLETICS

PLAY THE GAME

FIELD ATHLETICS

DAVID LEASE

BLANDFORD

A BLANDFORD BOOK

First published in the UK by Blandford
A Cassell Imprint
Cassell Plc, Villiers House,
41/47 Strand, London WC2N 5JE

Copyright © Text and Illustrations
1994 Blandford

Distributed in the United States by
Sterling Publishing Co., Inc.,
387 Park Avenue South, New York,
NY 10016-8810

Distributed in Australia by
Capricorn Link (Australia) Pty Ltd
2/13 Carrington Road, Castle Hill, NSW 2154

British Library Cataloguing-in-Publication Data
A catalogue entry for this title is available
from the British Library

ISBN 0-7137-2450-1

Typeset by Litho Link Ltd, Welshpool, Powys,
Wales

Printed and bound in Great Britain by The Bath
Press, Avon

**Frontispiece: The triple jump is a
combination of sprinting power,
explosive lift and balance.**

**Cover: Mike Powell achieves a world
record in the long jump.**

CONTENTS

ESSENTIAL NOTES

Coaching

Adults (over the age of 18) who wish to become qualified coaches should contact the British Athletic Federation, or the I.A.A.F. for information. In Great Britain and Northern Ireland there will be coach education courses in your area.

English

The English language is unfortunate in lacking a third-person singular personal pronoun that can refer to a person regardless of sex. In this book the male version has been used to represent both his and hers with apologies.

Safety

The notes in this book are written as a guide and are not intended to be a comprehensive document. Official instructions on the safety of track and field can be obtained from the British Athletic Federation and from The English Schools Athletic Association.

Drugs

Complete information on the subject of banned drugs and acceptable alternatives are produced by the British Athletic Federation and The Sports Council. Their addresses are in the chapter 'Useful Addresses'.

Acknowledgements

It would have been an impossible task to complete this book without the assistance of those people who have helped me. Some without knowing it! They are, in no particular order: The British Athletics Federation, Bruce Tulloh, Max Jones, Bruce Longden, Malcolm Arnold, Brad McStravick, Guntor Tidow, Vitaly Petrov, Gerhardt Schmolinsky, Tom McNab.

Special thanks must go to my understanding Secretary, Mary Emmerson.

INTRODUCTION

The dream of every athlete must be to win the Olympic Games with a world record performance in their chosen event. Such a winning performance represents the two avenues that motivate potential athletes. They are:

a) to win competitions

b) to improve one's personal best performance.

It is very important that athletes, especially young athletes, appreciate there are these two methods of gaining a sense of achievement. It would be nice, but unfortunately it is not always possible to win the competition. Most athletes would have a very unhappy career were it not for the aim of improving oneself. For example, there is only one winner of the London Marathon, but most of the competitors will return home happy that they have achieved a position or a time that they desired. Some will be delighted they simply completed the course! In this manner most competitors can be winners and this is one of the reasons people enjoy athletics competitions.

HISTORY OF
FIELD EVENTS

Field Athletics as we know them, with fibreglass vaulting poles, plastic foam landing areas, which allow high jumpers to hurl themselves over the bar head first and backwards, plastic run-ups, alloy javelins and 'Hi' or 'Low' spin discoi are a feature of the twentieth century. Nevertheless, they are a continuum of natural activities in which man has competed against man since time began.

Every society is proud of its best performers, as can be seen by the statues of discus throwers and spear throwers of ancient Greece, even the Neolithic cave paintings of athletes jumping over animals. Some form of field athletics is known to have existed as far back as the 19th century BC in the Tailteann Games, but the origin of organised track and field athletics is considered to be the founding of the Olympic Games in 776 BC, although no doubt these were a formalising of already existing activities. These games included the javelin and the discus. In those days the latter was thrown from a sloping platform, but we do not know how heavy it was. The games also included the long jump, and the athletes of the day were allowed to use hand held weights to assist them by swinging them at take-off. A form of multiple jump, similar to the triple jump, is also known to have existed, and one champion named Phaylus was known to have jumped 55 feet, five feet beyond the 'skamma' or landing area. He broke his leg in the process!

Other events are more recent in their first recordings. Shot putting was banned by statute by Edward III, who feared its popularity might lead to a decline in archery practise. Pole vaulting is thought to have been a natural way of clearing streams and dykes before becoming a formalised competition in 1839. However, there is some evidence in the Irish book of Leinster that it was included in those ancient Tailteann Games of 1829 BC.

The first modern Olympic Games were held in 1894, although in England organised meetings had been taking place throughout the century at Eton College, military establishments and Oxford and Cambridge. Eight years later, the International Amateur Athletic Federation was formed.

Women were first admitted to the games in 1928 but restricted to certain events; today, however, they may compete in almost all of them, most recently the Triple Jump.

A GUIDE TO
FIELD ATHLETICS

The aim of field athletics is to find out who can throw the furthest or jump the furthest – long or high. The organisers of world athletics are the International Amateur Athletics Federation, and the organisers of athletics in each country is that country's own athletic committee. In Great Britain it is the British Athletics Federation. It is their responsibility to ensure athletics happens and happens fairly. They provide the opportunities and the framework, such as rules governing the equipment allowed and the rules of competition. Athletics is organised on a local basis by athletic clubs and within schools. It is possible to find out if there is a club near you by telephoning your national federation. It is also possible to find out if there is a qualified coach of the event of your choice by telephoning the same number. (See 'Useful Addresses').

Each competition is run by judges appointed by the organisers. In all competitions, except the high jump and pole vault, the competitors are allowed between three and six individual trials in 'an order of competition' to be decided by the organisers. The high jumpers and pole vaulters are allowed three attempts at each height and are eliminated from the competition when they have incurred three consecutive failures. The results are recorded on a special card.

The following events are included.

JUMPS

Long Jump

This is a competition to see who can jump the furthest in one leap. A run-up of unlimited length is allowed, but the jumper must take off from behind a scratch line. A take-off board is provided, made of wood and set into the ground flush with the run-up. The front edge of this board marks the scratch line and soft material is laid in front of the line to help the judges ensure no one contravenes the rule. The jumper lands in a pit of sand, raked level with the run-up, and the jump is measured from the scratch line to the nearest identation made in the sand by any part of the jumper's body. Once the jump has been made the jumper must leave the sand pit under control and in front of the mark made. The jumper is not allowed any assistance such as springs in the shoes or weights in the hand.

Triple Jump (Hop, Step and Jump)

This is a competition to see who can cover the greatest distance in three bounds. These bounds must be continuous and made in the following order:

Long jump/triple jump landing area.

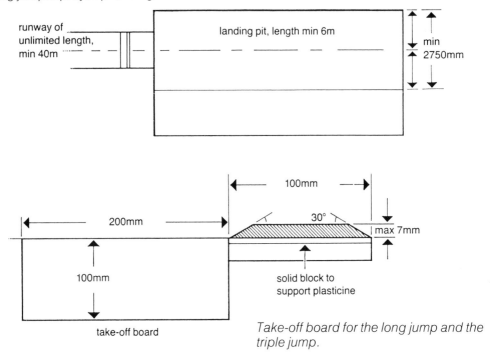

take-off board

Take-off board for the long jump and the triple jump.

Hop – the landing must be made on the same foot as was used to take off.
Step – the opposite foot must be used for landing as was used for take-off.
Jump – any controlled form of landing is acceptable.
The competition layout is the same as for the long jump, however the scratch line and take-off board will be set at an appropriate distance from the sand pit; this may be 9m, 11m or 13m depending on the standard of the competition.

High Jump

This is a competition to see who can jump the highest. A cross-bar is set on two uprights at ever increasing heights and the athlete that jumps over the bar set at the greatest height, without knocking it off, is declared the winner. A large flat area, known as the fan, is provided for an unlimited run up and a landing area or bed made of soft plastic foam provides safety on landing. There are very specific rules governing the size and composition of the landing areas allowed for competition.

The organisers will decide the starting height and the heights to which the bar will be raised. For example, the competition may start at 1.3 cm and then be raised a further 5 cm at the end of each round until everyone is eliminated. Each athlete is allowed three attempts at each height and is eliminated from the competition after incurring three consecutive failures. Athletes do not have to attempt each height nor do they have to take all three attempts at the same height. This can lead to tactics! However, they cannot go back down a height, nor can they attempt a height once they have declared they will pass.

The athlete must jump from one foot; two-footed jumps are not allowed. If the bar wobbles for a long time and finally falls it is the judge who decides whether the jump was fair or a failure. A jump is also considered a failure if the athlete touches the ground beyond the plane of the uprights without having cleared the bar first. The bar is always measured to the nearest centimetre below. Once the competition has been won within the heights set by the organisers the remaining jumper may set the bar at any height for the intention of breaking a record.

Pole Vault

The pole vault is a competition to see who can vault the highest with the aid of a pole. The pole must be made of one piece and can be of any material, and a rubber or plastic bung is allowed to be placed on the end of the pole to protect it. The pole vaulter can use sticky substances and up to two layers of tape to help that grip. The method of competition is the same as the high jump.

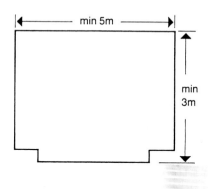

High jump landing area.

The run-up is unlimited and a sunken box 20 cm deep is built into the end of the run-up into which the vaulter places the pole at take-off. This stops the pole from slipping away. As in the high jump, a bar is placed on two uprights, but these can be moved up to 80 cm forwards or 40 cm backwards from the plane of the back of the box. A large, safe, landing area must be used and the size of this landing area is strictly

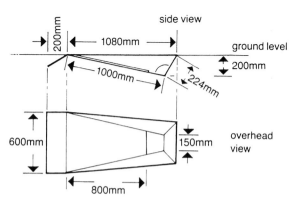

Pole vault sunken box into which the pole is planted.

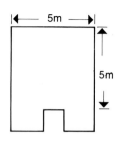

Pole vault landing area.

controlled by the athletic authorities. The very minimum size for competition is one that is 5 m square with added front extensions. Almost all international competitions are held on landing areas larger than this minimum size. The bed must also be thick enough to stop the vaulter 'bottoming' out or hitting the floor through the bed. The pole vaulter is not allowed to climb the pole, nor is he regarded as having vaulted until a performance is produced that touches the landing area or ground beyond plane of the back of the box by the vaulter or the vaulter's pole.

THROWS

All the throws are competitions to see who can throw the particular implement the furthest. Each implement must conform to the specifications laid down by the governing body, and there are different sizes for men, women and children in each

The great Sergei Bubka swings to handstand on his flexible pole before clearing the bar.

of the four disciplines. All fair throws are measured from the nearest part of the scratch line or circle rim to the thrower to the nearest point of contact the implement makes with the ground.

Javelin

The javelin is an updated spear, it has a point, a shaft and a cord grip. The throw must be made from a runway 4 m wide and 36.5 m long. At the front of the run-up is a curved scratch line which is extended out beyond the side lines by 75 cm. The thrower must not cross the curved scratch line or the extensions at any time and after the throw has been made must retire under control. The javelin is thrown into a sector of a radius of 29° which extends forward from the scratch line. The javelin does not have to stick in or even make a mark, but it does have to land point first.

No unconventional technique can be used to throw the javelin, it must be thrown in a particular fashion, one-handed and over the shoulder. Nor is the thrower allowed to turn his back to the direction of the throw while in the process of throwing, it cannot be hurled discus style for example.

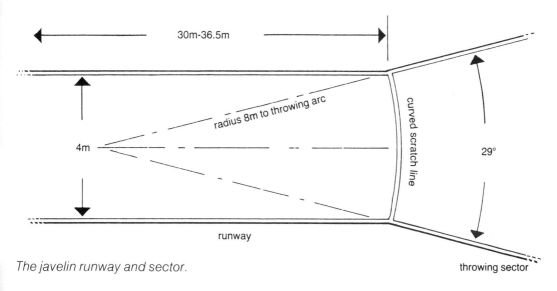

The javelin runway and sector.

Weights of competition javelins

	MEN	WOMEN
U13	400g	400g
U15	600g	600g
U17	700g	600g
U20	800g	600g
Senior	800g	600g

Lengths of competition javelins

600 g – 2.2 m
800 g – 2.6 m

There are a variety of 400 g javelins on the market for training and competition purposes, designed for use by children. Teachers and coaches should check that when the javelin is gripped correctly and the arm is held back at full length, the point of the javelin is not behind the head. In other words, check that the javelin is not too small for that particular child.

The Shot Putt

The shot is a fairly heavy metal ball which is putt or pushed from the confines of a concrete circle. The circle is 7 ft or 2.135 m

The shot put circle.

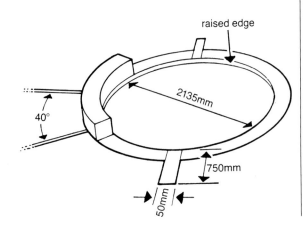

in diameter. It is edged with a metal rim that protrudes 20 mm above the level of the circle. At the front of the circle is a solid curved stop board made of wood, 10 cm high and approximately 11 cm wide and over 1.2 cm long. The shot is projected into a sector of 40°.

The thrower must begin the throw from a stationary position. The thrower must not touch any ground outside the circle, which includes the top of the metal rim and the top of the stop board. The thrower can enter the circle from any direction but must leave the circle from the rear half. The thrower must leave under control, and not until the shot has landed. The critical rule which defines shot putting says that the shot must be putt with one hand only, that it must be in close proximity with the chin and that it must not be taken back behind the line of the shoulders. The method of competition is the same as all throws.

Weights of competition shot

	MEN	WOMEN
U13	3.25kg	2.75kg
U15	4kg	3.25kg
U17	5kg	4kg
U20	6.25kg	4kg
Senior	7.26kg	4kg

Hammer

The hammer is a heavy metal ball, exactly the same as a shot, on the end of a wire. There is a swivel attaching the wire to the ball, and at the other end of the wire a triangular handle is attached.

The throw is made from a circle 2.135 m or 7 ft in diameter into a 40° sector. The circle is surrounded by a metal rim as in the shot and discus.

The athlete can wear gloves to protect the hands but these and the hammer are subject to strict rules. This is because the longer the distance between the athlete's shoulders and the hammer-head the

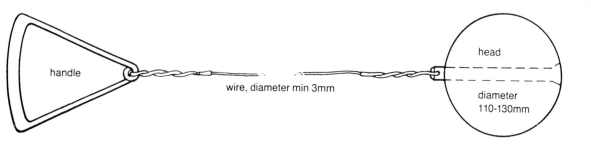

The hammer.

greater the leverage and the greater the advantage to the thrower. Long arms are acceptable but extra long wires and hooks on the end of gloves are not! The length of the hammer is measured from the inside of the handle to the tip of the ball.

There is no restriction on the method used to throw the hammer and throwers rotate up to four times inside the small circle with the hammer at arm's length. They do this to build up momentum, before hurling it backwards over their shoulder. The athlete is not allowed to touch the ground outside the circle until after the hammer has landed and then the athlete must leave the circle in a controlled manner. It is quite within the rules for the hammer to touch the ground during the process of a throw so long as the thrower does not stop. The thrower may stop and restart if the hammer has not touched the ground.

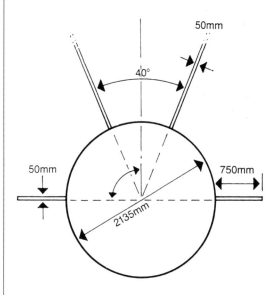

The hammer circle.

Weights and lengths of competition hammers

	MEN	WOMEN
U13	3.25kg	–
U15	4kg	–
U17	5kg	4kg
U20	6.25kg	4kg
Senior	7.26kg	4kg

Lengths of competition hammers (measured from inside grip)

For all weight categories

Minimum length = 117.5 cm
Maximum length = 121.5 cm

Discus

The discus is shaped rather like two plates stuck together face to face. It is heavier than one would think, being two kilos for a senior implement. If thrown properly it is aerodynamic and flies further than expected. It is made of wood or plastic and rimmed with metal.

The discus is thrown from a concrete circle 2.5 m in diameter. This circle has a metal rim as in the shot and hammer. The throw is made into a sector of 40°. Unlike the javelin

and shot there are no rules dictating the style of throw. The method adopted is a sling because no better alternative has been discovered due to the implement's weight and shape. As with the other throws made from a circle, the thrower must retire from the rear half, under control and not until the discus has landed.

Weights of competition discus

	MEN	WOMEN
U13	1kg	0.75kg
U15	1.25kg	1kg
U17	1.5kg	1kg
U20	1.75kg	1kg
Senior	2kg	1kg

Discus dimensions.

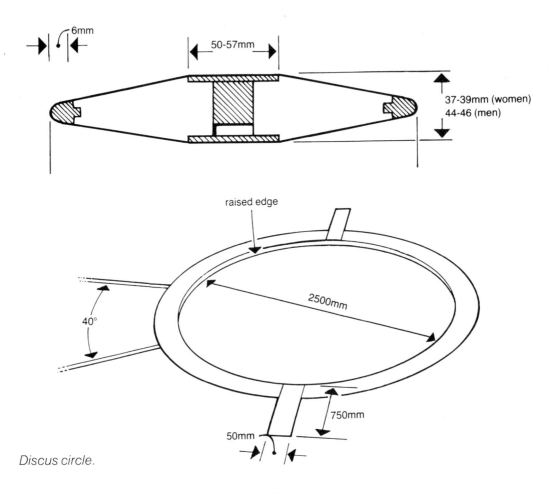

Discus circle.

JUMPING

All jumpers, including pole vaulters, try to extend the flight of their jumps by length or by height. They are limited by three vital ingredients which control the outcome and which come together at one critical moment, take-off. These three ingredients are:

1 The amount of forward or horizontal force. This is generated by the run-up. The faster you run the further it is possible to jump.

2 The amount of upward force. This depends on the athlete's jumping ability – spring.

3 The angle of take-off. Plentiful forward momentum and little upward momentum will result in a low angle to take-off and a long, low jump. Considerable upward momentum and little forward momentum will result in a high angle of take-off and a short, high jump.

One would be wise not to underestimate the amount of skill and training required to master these three seemingly simple requirements.

The jumps in track and field athletics therefore, have a number of common elements.

The run-up gains speed and culminates in two gathering strides, where the athlete makes a series of postural changes so that they may add the upward 'jump' effectively. Finally, there is the take-off when the athlete

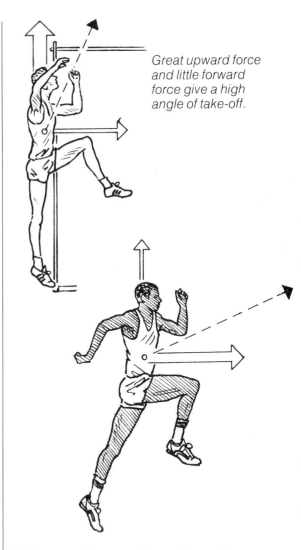

Great upward force and little forward force give a high angle of take-off.

Little upward force and great forward force give a low angle of take-off.

drives off the ground but also uses the other 'free' leg and arms vigorously to add momentum to the jump. Each jumper will vary these three elements depending on how they wish to fly through the air and also on their own physical attributes. Once take-off has taken place all the jumps have quite different techniques. It is also vital to appreciate that once take-off has happened nothing can be done to alter the athlete's flight path. (The pole vault is slightly different because the athlete is still in contact with the pole, but even so the ultimate height has been determined.)

Jumping events are sequential. The athlete can only clear the bar or make a good landing if the flight of the jump has been correct. The flight is only as good as the take-off and the take-off can only be effective if the run-up has been completed properly. It could be argued that the start of the run-up is the most important moment.

Jumping is all about generating as much force as possible through the take-off leg. However, it is vital the body is able to take the strain, rather like the fuselage of an aircraft must when the jet engines are turned to full pover. Imagine putting modern jet engines onto an old-fashioned, wood and canvas biplane! The same effect is created when strong legs drive into a weak torso. (See the chapter on training.)

LONG JUMP

Explanation of the event

Long jumping is the simplest activity of all the field events, only made complicated by the very high speeds at which it must be performed and by the quest for absolute perfection. The world's best are able to clear the width of the local high street with one bound! Jumping is one of the most natural of human activities and can be traced at least to our Neolithic ancestors who left cave drawings of people jumping

over animals which is an activity still practised in the South of France where the 'Running of the Bulls' is an annual event.

Now, in the twentieth century, long jumpers are allowed a run up of unlimited length but must take off from behind a specific line. This line is the front edge of the take-off board and is the line from which all jumps are measured. It is edged with a softer material, such as Plasticine, so that the athlete's footmark can be spotted should there be any doubt that he took off from the correct place. The jumper lands in soft sand and the jump is measured to the nearest mark, made in the sand, to the take-off board. The athlete must not walk back through the sand-pit but exit from a point in front of the landing made.

Principles of Long Jumping

The first objective of the long jumper is to achieve the best possible flight path for the longest possible jump. This is met by mustering as much speed as possible during the run-up and then adding to it vertical lift to produce the best angle of take-off. Speed of approach plus lift at take-off determine how far the athlete's centre of gravity will fly. Nothing that is done in the air can alter this fact. The second objective is to ensure that the body is in the correct position at landing to cut the sand at the furthest possible distance. If a long jumper is able to land with their feet well out in front of them, then they will have made the most of their take-off.

Clearly, the most important part of long jumping is therefore the approach run and the take-off. The landing cannot even be considered until the athlete is airborne and will be dependant on whether the flight is well balanced. Possible long jumpers are therefore advised to spend most of their training on run-up and take-off. However, a good take-off is likely to set up some forward rotation and should the athlete do nothing about the rotation while in the air they could fall forward on landing. Not to be advised, if only because it cuts down the distance achieved. Considerable practice is required to achieve the correct aerial movements but they must not, as has unfortunately happened in the past, overshadow the first objective, that of making a fast take-off with good lift.

THE LONG JUMP TECHNIQUE

The Run-Up

This should be completed with good sprinting technique to give the athlete the fastest speed that can be negotiated at take-off. It must also ensure the athlete arrives at the correct point on the take-off board. Consequently, it must be consistent to give the athlete any chance of competing with confidence. By tradition, long jumpers tend to use a run up of an uneven number of strides because it means they move their take-off foot first and can therefore concentrate on it. However there is no necessity to run this way. The length of run-up is important because the athlete must be at the correct speed at take-off, neither lacking in speed because the run-up was too short nor slowing down because the run-up was too long. Most senior long jumpers find a run-up of about 21 strides satisfactory and junior jumpers are generally happy with run-ups that more or less coincide with their age: 13 years old = 13 strides, 14 years old = 13 or 15 strides.

A standing start to the run-up is the best to ensure consistency of length but, once again, some athletes find it difficult to relax from a standing start. Consequently, after all methods have been learned the mature athlete should choose a run up that allows them to demonstrate the best of their ability.

Take-Off

The gather strides into take-off are a complex series of movements capable of tying the cleverest of athletes into knots if analysed too deeply! Fortunately, they are a very natural series of movements. The athlete is advised to concentrate on his rhythm, da-da-da-de-da, maintaining momentum and keeping the hips high. However, this last point is actually in direct contrast with what actually happens. While the athlete concentrates on the *sensations* of the movements the coach or scientist can concentrate on the *actual* movements which show that during these strides the centre of gravity will sink and the knees bend to prime the powerful muscles of the legs. The penultimate stride is usually slightly longer than normal and the last stride slightly shorter. The take-off foot should be planted in front of the centre of gravity. This allows the hips to be raised from a low position in the last stride through to a high position at take-off, allowing the athlete to gain height and a good angle of take-off.

The athlete should also assist the take-off by considerably accelerating the 'free limbs'. The non take-off leg is swung though and upwards vigorously and both arms are driven in an exaggerated running action, one forward, one backward but both upward against the braced take-off leg. Finally, the take-off leg is straightened explosively. The take-off must set up and create a balanced flight where the athlete is in complete control of his movements.

The Flight

Long levers rotate slower than short levers, therefore, the forward rotation set up by take-off can be slowed while in flight by extending the body to its fullest. The technique long jumpers use employing this method is known as the 'Hang'.

It is possible to set up counter-rotation by

The long jump 'hang' technique.

The long jump 'hitchkick' technique.

cycling one's arms and legs, exactly as done with the arms to stop one falling off a cliff edge. The technique employing this cycling action is known as a 'Hitchkick'. Athletes usually make one complete aerial stride of the 'free' leg. The take-off leg is simply brought through to the front – half a cycle. This sequence constitutes a one and a half hitchkick. (This technique is also called a one stride hitchkick). Advanced men have been known to employ two and a half cycles – one and a half cycles of the free leg and one cycle of the take-off leg! (Also known as a two stride hitchkick). The arms are cycled forwards in synchronisation with the legs. It is important to realise that once the cycling stops the original rotation returns, and that this action only serves to set up a better position for landing. It cannot have any effect on the path of the centre of gravity as this was determined at take-off.

One of the essential parts of the flight is to adopt the correct position on approach to landing. The arms should be long and above the head.

Landing

The most efficient landing is one where the feet cut the sand as far away from the take-off board as possible. To achieve this the legs must be near horizontal and not drop. This position is achieved not through strength but by swinging the arms from above the head downwards and backwards so that they finish behind the athlete. Newton's third Law of Motion states 'that to every action there is an equal and opposite reaction'; the reaction to the downward and backward swing of the arms is a forward and upward lift of the legs. However, timing is critical.

After cutting the sand with the feet the long jumper attempts to buckle the legs and slide into the hole created, without disturbing the sand behind with any part of the body, either by sitting back or by allowing a lazy hand to spoil an otherwise good performance.

Carl Lewis concentrates as he prepares for landing.

Learning The Event

It is probably best to concentrate on the work done on the ground and to simplify the flight by ignoring possible forward rotation. This rotation is likely to be relatively insignificant with the beginner because they will not be using great force and consequently not jumping very far.

A basic jump should include:

A correct run up.
A correct take-off.
A correct landing.

The aerial element should be limited to simply bringing the take off-leg through to join the non take-off leg (the free leg). This basic technique for beginners is known as a 'Stride' jump.

Progressions to learning a stride jump

1   All forms of jumping, hopping and skipping should be learned with good posture. The arm actions should be of a single arm shift, that is one arm forward and one arm backwards as in a natural running action. These activities should not be practised for distance but for correct execution. The coach or teacher can give marks out of ten for style!

2   Jumps over low hurdles with one and later three strides in between for correct rhythm. The distances should be comfortable to suit the individual athlete.

Long jump stride jump sequence.

3 With a short run, step up onto a beat board, or low, sturdy box top and jump into the sand. The added height of the board or box will give the athlete the feeling of lift at take-off and also more time in the air to practise the correct stride jump movement.

4 Establish a short run-up by trial and error methods.

5 Practise the full jump.

6 Variations can be to jump over low elastic bars or sand castles and to try to head a foam ball suspended at an appropriate height above the sand pit.

Special Safety

1 Always dig the sand to ensure a soft landing and to ensure nothing has become buried such as stones or glass.

2 Always jump from a non-slip surface.

TRIPLE JUMP

Explanation of the Event

The triple jump is unique in track and field in that it is not a 'simple' activity, instead it is a rather contrived, combination activity. It is none the less a very natural series of movements, as are all track and field activities initially, although at international level most events have been developed

well beyond movements that could be called natural. A multi-jump competition was held as long ago as the ancient Greek Olympics, but we cannot be certain that the sequence of hop, step, jump, was the same as we know it today. Rules have changed even in the last hundred years; indeed, the first winner of the modern Olympics, James Connolly, won with two hops and a jump with all the take-offs being from his strongest leg. In the competitions of today he would be disqualified.

Principles of Triple Jumping

The main problem faced by triple jumpers is that of maintaining momentum. Momentum is generated during the run-up, and good jumpers take off in such a way as to lose as little forward momentum as possible, but each take-off and landing inevitably causes the athlete to slow down and consequently lose distance. Unfortunately, the triple jump has three take-offs.

The triple jumper has discovered two methods to conserve momentum through all phases of the jump:

1   The athlete does not take off at the angle which will produce the longest possible hop but keeps the flight parabola rather lower, like a pebble someone has 'skimmed' across a pond.

2   The athlete uses an 'active' landing and take-off action at each ground contact. The landing can be very jarring and inefficient unless the athlete reaches with the landing leg and then claws the ground backwards as contact is made. This action is the same as that used by the active leg when 'scooting' along on a skateboard or scooter.

THE TRIPLE JUMP TECHNIQUE

Run-Up

The triple jump run-up is no different to that of the long jump and therefore you are advised to read that chapter. However, it is important to generate the 'optimum' amount of speed for the triple jump take-off, which may be different to the maximum speed possible. Taking off is reasonably easy but unless the athlete is experienced and well-conditioned (strong) the forces generated at take-off may be too great for one leg to accept on landing.

The Hop

This part of the event should be completed as fast as possible. While the athlete should sense a flat footed contact with the take-off board it should in actual fact be slightly heel first. The athlete will gather for the jump in the final two strides and take off driving the other knee vigorously upwards along with the opposite arm. The take-off leg is extended explosively and the best angle for take-off is thought to be between 15–18°. During the flight, which must be balanced, the take-off knee is picked up so that the thigh is parallel to the ground. The athlete is then in a position to reach and strike so as to engage the 'active' landing and take-off for the second phase.

The Step

Take-off should be completed at an angle between 13 and 15° to achieve the best results. The athlete can use a single or double arm shift but must drive the free thigh vigorously so that once again it becomes parallel with the ground. The athlete often appears to demonstrate a splits position in the air when the action is completed properly.

hop take-off   step take-off   jump take-off

The three take-offs in the triple jump. Note the positions of the arms and the varying angle of take-off.

The Jump

Momentum at this stage is decreasing rapidly however much the athlete strives to maintain it. Therefore, the take-off angle should be much higher than the other two phases – between 20 and 24°. A double arm shift should be used and, as in all jumps, the free knee should be driven hard and the take-off leg extended explosively. The jump, if long enough, can be completed with any of the recognised long jump techniques. However, beginners are unlikely to have enough time in the air for such luxuries, so a 'stride' or 'hang' style is adequate. The aim of the flight is to adopt a position in the air that will allow for an effective landing. That is, with legs fully extended in front and with the arms high above the head so that they can be swung downwards and backwards. This action lifts the feet just prior to landing because of the principle of Newton's third Law of Motion 'To every action there is an equal and opposite reaction'.

Rhythm

The rhythm of the sequence of the three jumps is vitally important to gain good distances. The athlete should attempt to make the flight time of each jump more or less equal and should therefore sense a TAA – TAA – TAA timing. Beginners often demonstrate a huge hop, a very short step followed by a long jump. This pattern has been proved to be highly inefficient. In reality, the best distance ratio for a good triple jumper should be approximately:

Hop 37%   Step 30%   Jump 34%

Arm Actions

Jumpers are able to help their performances by swinging their arms at take-off. The arms can either be swung together (a double arm shift), or they can be swung one forward and one backward as in a natural running action (a single arm shift). At take-off this arm swing adds lift, or upward momentum, to the athlete. In a single arm shift even the arm lifted backwards is being driven upwards and consequently adds lift. A two arm shift is probably more effective but unfortunately takes longer to complete. The hop needs to be completed at the greatest possible speed and therefore all good triple jumpers use a single arm shift to aid the hop take-off. The jumper will slow and is in a position to use either arm action for the step take-over. However, by the time the athlete takes off for the jump, momentum will have been reduced to such an extent that any acceptable method will be required to maximise that jump, so a two arm shift is likely to be best.

Learning the Event

Youngsters should learn a whole variety of little hops, skips and jumps and gain experience of many combinations of movements. It should not be assumed that children will learn these without instruction. Games such as hopscotch are ideal.

Progressions towards learning the triple jump

1   From standing, practise a hop. Practise both feet.

2   From standing, practise a hop followed by a long, high step. Ensure the distance, height and rhythm of both are the same. It is useful to have lines drawn on the ground as a guide for distance. (These lines can be useful to ensure youngsters do not jump too far. Landing on one foot can be very stressful as the forces involved can be extremely high and therefore practices must be controlled.) It is wise not to teach the jump phase until the hop step can be completed correctly to ensure the correct rhythm.

3   The complete hop, step and jump can be practised into the sand pit. Practise from standing and then from a short run-up.

Triple jump sequence.

4   The reaching and pawing action needs explanation. Practice by stepping rather than hopping, results have been found to be better this way. Ensure 'flat foot' contacts.

5   Full run-ups should be treated with sensitivity until the athlete is adequately conditioned.

Special Safety

Good, firm shoes are important to the triple jumper. They should be stable enough to ensure the ankle is not turned over, especially during training. They should also have strong enough soles along their length so that they do not buckle. Special competition shoes are available but the athlete should ensure that any hopping or bounding practices should be done in good trainers with wide, stable heels. Shoes with worn-down heels must be avoided.

HIGH JUMP

Explanation of the Event

High jumping has probably seen more technique changes than any other athletic event. This is not just because people have been imaginative in their response to jump over a bar set as high as possible but because the priority has been to survive the fall on the other side! In the past, rules have been set by the governing bodies to ensure just that. In the first instance, The Highland Games provided no more than grass as a landing site. Consequently, high jumpers used techniques that landed them feet first or at least hands and feet together like the 'Scissors', 'Western Roll' and the 'Eastern Cut Off'. Sand eventually replaced grass and peat or sawdust replaced sand, giving a much softer and consequently safer landing which allowed athletes to jump with rather less concern. This permitted the development of quite an advanced technique, the 'Straddle', which is still occasionally used. Finally, plastic foam

landing areas arrived and governing bodies felt confident enough to allow high jumpers to clear the bar head first. It was not long after this rule change that Dick Fosbury of the U.S.A. and Debbie Brill of Canada responded with a technique that has become known as the 'Fosbury Flop'.

The Principles of Jumping Flop Style

High jumping can be compared to throwing a stiff bamboo cane, end-on, at a concrete floor. It bounces! High jumpers use this same principle by running as fast as they can control and bouncing off their take-off leg. The leg does bend at the knee but the muscles contract as fast as possible in the recoil to propel the athlete upwards.

THE HIGH JUMP TECHNIQUE

The Flop Technique

This has developed from the early scissors technique – a simple scissors kick. Scissors jumpers run at the bar at an acute angle, take off from their outside foot and swing the inside leg upwards to clear the bar in a sitting position. They land on the swinging 'free leg'.

One of the main reasons Flop jumpers are able to clear a bar set at a greater height is not because they jump higher but because they have perfected the efficiency of the clearance. A Flopper can clear a bar despite their centre of gravity passing under it. A Scissors jumper must elevate their centre of gravity well above the bar. Top class male high jumpers usually find they can jump about 30 cm higher with the Flop than the Scissors. The technique is similar to the Scissors in that the jumper

The scissors jump.

takes off on the outside foot. The inside or free leg is swung vigorously, along with the arms to help gain lift. The athlete then completes a half twist to clear the bar backwards, head leading. The landing is made on the back.

Flop Run-up

The run-up is essential to gain speed which can be translated into height but it also has other purposes:

To arrive at the correct place to clear the middle of the bar (the lowest part.)

To develop enough rotation for the athlete to complete the half twist while in the air so that they may clear the bar on their back.

JUMPING

Consequently, the final three to five strides of the run-up are curved to create the required rotation. The run-up is shaped as a 'J' but the amount of curve and the length of the run-up are individually tailored to the athlete's ability with 9 strides usually being ample to generate the right amount of speed. The run-up should be completed with a well practised sprinting action leaning into the curve from the ankles. As take-off is approached the athlete must use the gather steps to insure that the take-off foot is well ahead of the body (producing a leaning back position) and will touch the ground heel first before rolling onto the ball of the foot. The take-off foot should be pointing more or less towards the direction the athlete will travel. It is an important safety point that the foot is not turned outwards as this can result in injury to the ankle or knee, a good pointer is the far upright. As a result of running around the curve the athlete should be leaning away from the bar.

Take-Off

At take-off the jumping leg is straightened so vigorously and the free knee is brought through so fast that the torso must be firm and strong to accept these forces. It is important that the athlete concentrates on jumping upwards and is not impatient to clear the bar. The free knee should continue to be driven upwards until bar clearance begins.

Clearance

When the time comes to clear the bar the athlete should lift the hips rather than throw the head backwards. Good high jumpers are able to sight the bar for at least the early part of the clearance. To complete the clearance the head should be lifted to look at the feet; the equal and opposite reaction to this movement is that the knees and feet will move to meet the head and be lifted clear of the bar.

standing

vertical jump

scissors jump

flop

*A comparison of the various high jump techniques shows how a 'flopper' can clear a higher bar – the flopper's center of gravity (x) passes **below** the bar, whilst a scissor jumper must raise the centre of gravity **above** the bar.*

FIELD · ATHLETICS

Learning the Event

Into a well-dug sand pit with stands and an elastic cross bar:

1 Run directly at the bar and jump over the bar, set at a low height, landing on two feet. This ensures the correct take-off foot contact.

2 Run 3–5 strides from an acute angle and 'scissors' the bar. Practise from both sides to discover your favourite side. Land on your feet.

Onto an official landing mat:

1 Scissors to sit on the mat facing forward. Repeat, but land progressively facing more towards the bar until you can complete a 90° turn.

2 From a two-foot take-off complete a gentle back drop onto the mat. Land on

a rounded back and not on the upper part of the back or neck. Progress gradually until you can perform it over an elastic bar.

3 From a short approach attempt the complete flop over a low elastic bar.

All practices must be completed with controlled movements.

Special Safety

Always jump from a firm and non-slip surface; jumping from wet grass is dangerous.

Always plant the take-off foot in natural alignment with the direction of the jump. Pointing the foot towards the far upright is a reasonable target. Teachers and Coaches must watch closely for a turned out foot and stop it.

High jump sequence.

Always use suitable footwear – a well fitting jumping shoe with heel spikes on the take-off foot is essential for serious jumpers.

Always use a recognised high jump bed for the flop technique.

Always check the landing area for gaps underneath the cover.

Always acquire instruction before attempting the flop.

POLE VAULT

Explanation of the Event

Pole vaulting is arguably the most spectacular of all the track and field events and leading exponents regularly vault over heights that equate to the roof of a two-storey building. Early vaults were made over canals or over a cross-bar to land on grass. Poles were made of wood, usually ash, and originally the pole had prongs to stop the end sliding about on the ground. Now a metal trough or box 20 cm deep is used, and the uprights are allowed to be moved (within reason) to suit the modern pole vaulter. Initially, bamboo poles were used, with the landing being made into sand. This was later replaced by sawdust and now specially designed plastic foam mats are used. Pole vaulters have always sought flexible, whippy poles to help them and current poles are made of fibreglass or carbon fibre. Sergey Bubka, a Ukrainian, dominated the event throughout the 1980s and has to date broken the world record more times than any other athlete in any event!

The Principles of Pole Vaulting

Pole vaulters gain height by two methods:

1 They hold the pole as high as possible. This is achieved by running as fast as possible and vigorously pushing the pole upwards to the vertical at take-off. Tall athletes obviously have a distinct advantage over shorter colleagues. Poles that bend also assist the athlete considerably in the quest for a high grip. When the pole bends it allows the weight of the athlete to stay near the ground for much longer, but this only works, of course, if the pole is strong enough to straighten in the final stages! In recent years, flexible poles have allowed athletes to increase their heights of grip by over a metre and are the main reason for the improvement of the world record from the early 1960's to the present day.
(Note: While pole vaulters are allowed to use poles of unlimited length, it is vital at first, to err on the side of caution and not hold higher than is safe.)

2 The pole vaulter elevates himself above his grip on the pole. Outstanding exponents are able to clear a cross bar as much as 1.20 m above their hand hold. This part of the vault is pure gymnastics and is aided by the 'catapult' recoil from the plastic pole. The most critical rule to be observed is that the body weight must be above the shoulders before the pole recoils. This means the pole vaulter is more than half way to being completely upside down while the pole is at its biggest bend. Consequently, the body is fired upwards rather than thrown forwards and downwards.

Done it! The short journey back to earth after a successful jump is a joyful one for the athlete.

POLE VAULT TECHNIQUE

Pole vault technique divides itself neatly into two parts.

Run-up to take-off

Carrying the Pole

We have already noted that taking off at the highest possible speed is essential for a high vault. However, carrying a pole is a considerable inconvenience, and this inconvenience must be kept to a minimum. The pole is held with the favourite hand at the top and the other hand between 40 and 60 cm lower down. The thumbs and forefingers of each hand should be to the top.

Carrying the pole.

Take-Off

At the moment of take-off the top of the top hand should be vertically aligned with the front of the take-off foot. The aim is to jump as a long jumper and at the same time to push the pole to the vertical. It is important that the vaulter drives from the tip of his toe up and through the top of his chest. The vaulter helps the magnitude of his jump, as do all jumpers, by vigorously driving his non take-off leg upwards.

Take-Off to Landing (Including Bar Clearance).

This phase is pure gymnastics. The pole vaulter has two immediate jobs to complete. One is to bend the pole and to ensure that he penetrates towards the landing area. The second is to ensure he is well on the way to getting upside down before the pole starts to recoil. There will always be personal interpretations to the challenges set, especially as physiques and abilities vary. However, during this initial 'flight' phase the vaulter begins by pushing the pole from take-off, chest leading and free knee driving. The take-off leg is held back until the critical moment when the swing should begin. Then the back leg is swung vigorously and the vaulter tucks or pikes to invert himself. The very best competitors attempt to complete all these movements with straight arms because it helps both to bend the pole and also to produce the best swing to upside-down, although in the moments immediately after take-off the lower arm tends to act rather like a shock absorber. (By straight arms I mean athletically straight, not locked). This movement is virtually identical to the movement called a 'short circle to hand stand' performed by Olympic gymnasts on the high bar. It is, therefore, not surprising that most of the leading pole vaulters practise Olympic gymnastics as part of their training.

At the beginning of the run-up most pole vaulters like to carry the pole as vertically as possible. As the run-up progresses they allow the pole to fall gradually until, two strides from take-off, the pole is exactly horizontal. This moment represents the beginning of the pole plant. However, it is important to appreciate that the run-up, pole plant and take-off are one continuous movement.

The pole plant is a sequence of well rehearsed movements designed to transfer the pole from the carrying position to an overhead position ready for take off. The right hand should move from above the hip to directly overhead in a straight line, passing the forehead on the penultimate foot contact. Both hands should push the pole upwards together.

The pole vault take-off.

The swing to upside-down is only complete when the pole vaulter is completely in line with the pole. This upside-down position is held for an agonisingly long period of time from the pole vaulter's point of view, although in reality it is hardly a second of time. No one should underestimate the confidence required, nor the accuracy of the knowledge of one's ability: this movement is the product of dedicated training and expert coaching! As the pole completes its whip-like recoil the pole vaulter pulls with both arms which propels him upwards from the pole and causes him to complete half a turn. This allows the bar to be cleared in a rainbow-like arch.

This arch position must be held with the head down and the thumbs turned in, which turns the elbows out and helps the vaulter clear the bar smoothly. There should then be a 'joyous' fall of up to some five metres onto the athlete's back. It is very unwise to land on any other part of the body, especially the feet, where ankles can be twisted, or the seat, which can result in whiplash.

Learning the Event

The pole vault should be learnt on soft dry grass using a short pole.

1   The pole should be held with the favourite hand at forehead height and the other hand 30/40 cm lower. Thumbs and forefingers should be uppermost. From 2 to 3 strides practise a boy scout vault (a short swing on the pole). Land on both feet, together.

2   In further efforts, the right-handed vaulter should ensure that the right hand is uppermost, that he swings on the right side of the pole and that he takes off from the left foot.

3   Hold the pole vertically and as high as possible with the top hand while standing on tip toes. With this grip practise swinging on the pole but hanging from it with your top arm remaining straight.

Transfer to a well dug sand pit.

4 Repeat no.3 placing the pole into the sand pit and practise swinging on the pole for distance. It will be necessary to grip some 20 cm higher as the pole will sink into the sand.

5 VERY GRADUALLY, 2 cm at a time, raise the grip up the pole. It is vital not to hurry this as too high a grip can result in a fall onto the back, which will be most uncomfortable!

Practise SWINGING FOR DISTANCE, gradually building up confidence.

6 Add a 180° twist just before landing.

7 Try to vault over an elastic cross-bar set well back. It is unwise to attempt higher than one metre.

8 Once accomplished, transfer to the pole vault area proper. Ensure an accurate run-up before attempting any vaults into the landing area.

Special Safety

1 Always practise under supervision.

2 Do not rush the progressions.

3 Always start at the beginning each time.

4 Avoid slippery conditions.

5 Always check the facilities for safety.

6 Err on the side of caution especially where grip heights are concerned.

7 Look after fibreglass poles carefully. They are thin and may chip or crack if allowed to fall, and future vaults may cause them to break while the pole vaulter is airborne. Therefore, always have someone to catch the pole.

Pole vault sequence.

SPRINTING TECHNIQUE

Sprinting plays such an important part in the jumping events, and the javelin, that it is worthy of a short section of its own.

Each of the jumps is dependent on the speed of approach and the posture of that approach. The world's best long jumper has been known to achieve a speed in excess of 12 m per second during the final stride before take-off and even pole vaulters carrying the pole occasionally reach over 10 m per second. In fact it could be said that speed is the limiting factor, at least in the horizontal jumps. Therefore, athletes need to work extremely hard to achieve a technique that will enable them to run as fast as possible.

Running is a natural action but athletes train to exaggerate that action, although there are only two ways of improving their running. These two ways are:

1   To cut down the time each stride takes (stride rate).

2   To increase each stride length, without slowing stride rate.

The Sprinting Action

Posture   The athlete should feel as tall as possible. The feeling is one of brushing the ceiling with the crown of the head. In particular, the hips should be as far from the ground as possible. The back should be upright but the shoulders low and wide. There is little difference between the instructions of the sprint coach and the piano teacher!

Arm Action   The arms should move backwards and forwards rather than across the body where excessive rotation will slow the athlete down. The arm action is to off set rotation set up by the leg action. Short levers move faster than long levers so the arms should be bent to approximately 90° at the elbows.

Leg Action   Running is a pushing action. The foot makes contact with the ground just as the body is about to pass over it. Once in contact with the ground the leg straightens backwards through the feet and pushes the body forward. Once the push has been completed the leg must recover to repeat the action. As already highlighted, short levers move faster than long so the leg

The sprinting approach.

must be tucked tight to be brought through quickly. Sprinters strive to get the knee high in front of them at the end of this recovery action because it helps to increase their stride length.

Sprinters must repeat this action at high speed over and over again. (Top class 100 m sprinters usually take about 43–45 strides to complete 100 m).

RELAXATION is essential to the runner if very fast sprinting is desired. Not only should the movements be performed correctly they must be done without the body tightening up. White knuckles and hunched sholders spell disaster for someone wishing to run fast or jump a long way.

EACH ATHLETE IS A UNIQUE PERSON and while techniques can be recommended, the style with which they are performed will often be quite different. Ultimately, the aim must be to harness that unique talent special to the athlete. This is why world champions frequently do not have text book actions. They do not have text book physiques nor do they have a text book coordination system inside their body. Sometimes they may not have been taught particularly well!

Training for Sprinting

Improving stride rate

Movements that represent part of the sprinting action should be isolated and practised to ensure a perfect action. These are then practised faster and faster before being reintroduced to the full action. These practises are either called technique drills or speed drills.

Improving stride length

Mobility exercises must be practised frequently, at least two to three times per week, to increase the range of movement which will allow a longer stride to take place.

Technique should be practised twice a week to ensure the movements are correct.

Strength can be improved by circuit training, weight training, hopping and bounding to drive the body forward. The torso must also be strengthened so that it does not crumple under the stress of powerful leg thrusts.

Special running exercises can also be performed to gradually encourage the athlete to adopt a progressively longer stride.

THROWING

All throwers try to extend the flight of their implements. They are limited by a number of vital ingredients which control the outcome and which come together at one critical moment – the moment of delivery. These ingredients are:

1   The amount of force that can be generated. This force must result in the fastest possible speed that can be transferred to the implement and is a combination of the athlete's personal speed and strength. The athlete trains many hours to improve these.

2   The range over which this force can be applied. This is why the hammer thrower using three turns is able to impart more force than one that only uses one turn.
Therefore: DISTANCE = FORCE × RANGE (TIME)

3   The height of release. The higher above the ground the implement is released the further the implement will travel.

4   The angle at which the implement is released. Everyone realises that a bullet fired from a gun will travel further if fired at 45° than if fired parallel to the ground. The principle is the same for throwing. However, while 45° might theoretically be the best angle to 'fire' a shot, discus, javelin or hammer this angle is slightly decreased by the height from above the ground at which it is released. Aerodynamic factors also affect the angle of throwing and require the implement to be thrown at a lower angle than the suggested norm of 45°. While the shot and hammer have aerodynamic qualities similar to a house brick, the discus in particular and the javelin are designed to make the most of any flight properties that might exist. The angle at which they are thrown will therefore differ.

Because of these principles all throwers have found there are common elements which produce the best throws. These are:

1   LOW TO HIGH – All throwers start the final 'strike' with the implement low down and deliver it at the highest possible level.

2   TRANSFER OF WEIGHT/BALANCE – It is only possible to throw successfully from an 'on balance' position. From this position the back leg drives the body and implement upwards and over the front foot.

3   BRACED OPPOSITE SIDE – The throwing side of the body which is responsible for delivering the throw is worked against a solid support provided by the opposite side of the body.

4 SEQUENCE OF MOVEMENT – All good throws are delivered by initiating the movement with the largest and most powerful muscles of the body in the upper legs and lower trunk. The throw is completed by the lighter, faster muscles of the limbs and finally the hands and feet. This results in the body starting the movement relatively slowly but accelerating it so that it is completed at the fastest possible speed.

All great performers look as though they make their particular skill look easy. This applies to all activities, whether jumping, playing soccer or playing the piano. This is because they have balance, timing and rhythm. These qualities are the product of natural ability and many hours of correct practice. They are also essential qualities required to throw well.

THE JAVELIN

Explanation of the Event

One of the most exhilarating sights of modern athletics is to sit behind the javelin throwers and watch them launch the javelins into the sky. It can be compared to watching aircraft leave the runway at a major airport, for the power applied and the resulting flight seem to parallel one another. In recent years javelin throwers have 'out thrown' the stadium's available space; over the length of a football pitch has been achieved and as a result the dimensions of the javelins have been changed causing them to fall to earth slightly sooner. Nevertheless, distances near the length of the football pitch are achieved and the event is no less spectacular. High jumpers and pole vaulters who compete at the far end of the stadium are, however, a little safer now.

The javelin is, of course, no more than a development on the spears used by ancient man to kill game for food. Our forefathers would be most jealous of the distances we can now throw, which are due not only to a greater understanding of techniques and training methods but also to the science and technology that have been applied to the construction of javelins. Javelins are designed to be as aerodynamic as the rules allow and companies that produce javelins are as competitive as the throwers themselves.

No unusual techniques are allowed. The thrower must throw from above the shoulder and is not allowed to turn his back to the direction of the throw. This is because throwers experimented, very successfully, with a rotational technique in the early 1960's. The distances achieved were excellent but the direction the javelin flew proved to be dangerously erratic and therefore the technique was outlawed.

Basic Principles of Throwing the Javelin

The best throws are those that adhere to the basic principles which are:

1 The javelin should be released at the greatest possible speed.

2 The javelin should be released at the most efficient angle. Were it a stone and released at ground level, 45° would be perfect. However it is aerodynamic and the thrower's arm might be as high as 8 ft from ground level. Therefore, the angle of release will be lower than 45°.

3 The javelin should be released as high above the ground as possible.

THE JAVELIN TECHNIQUE (for a right handed thrower)

Gripping the javelin

We have already highlighted that top class javelin throwers throw the javelin at incredibly high speeds. Therefore, the grip on the javelin that transfers all the force produced to the javelin must be extremely secure. However, security is not the only consideration and an arm moving with such force must be protected from injury. Throwers usually adopt one of the following three options.

'V' Grip

This version allows the javelin to lie along the length of the palm of the hand and is therefore the least likely to cause injury to the elbow joint. The elbow is a hinge joint and when it is straightened in its correct line of working everything is fine. Problems occur when stress is put across the hinge. The 'V' grip also allows two fingers to be placed behind the cord on the javelin enabling the thrower to derive plenty of purchase on the javelin at the moment of throwing. It is therefore an ideal option, although unfortunately, some people find it rather uncomfortable.

Middle finger grip

Once again the javelin lies along the palm of the hand but is gripped by the middle finger and thumb. This is a particularly popular grip and there is little compromise on the ideal basic principles. Also, this grip allows spin or rifling to be imparted to the javelin, theoretically helping it to fly further.

At the moment of his world record throw, Steve Backley is a model of balance and power.

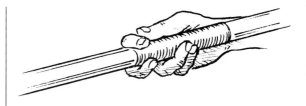

The javelin V grip.

The javelin middle finger grip.

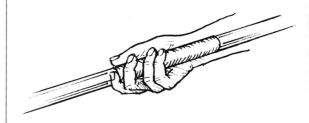

The javelin forefinger grip.

Forefinger grip

The forefinger is placed behind the binding of the javelin and sometimes the thumb is as well. However, when the thumb is added it can lead to elbow injury as the javelin lies slightly across the palm of the hand. Some leading throwers with strong forefingers employ this method with great success as they find it very comfortable even though only one finger is responsible for the throw. It also allows plenty of spin to be placed on the javelin.

The run-up

The javelin is carried high above the shoulder with the palm of the hand facing upwards. It is very important that the palm remains upwards throughout the throw both for the best result and to avoid injury. The simplest and arguably the most effective run-up is one that follows the following nine stride pattern:

Four running strides   Starting from a standing start (to ensure accuracy). The first step should be taken with the left foot. These four strides must be well balanced and progressively increase in speed.

Two running strides   Withdrawing the javelin. The sensation that should be felt by the athlete during these two strides is one of running away from the javelin and leaving it behind. The movement of the shoulders and arm begin at the very natural moment when the athlete steps forward with the left foot for the third time. The movement is continued gradually and completed before the thrower moves into the final three strides. Turning the shoulders sideways and taking the javelin back so that the arm is held straight behind increases the range over which the thrower can apply force when the actual throw begins. The arm should remain above the level of the shoulders and should be 'athletically' straight, not rigidly straight or 'locked out'.

Three throwing strides   The final three strides are completed with a specific throwing rhythm. This is difficult to explain verbally but musically the rhythm of the feet beats dum, deee da! The penultimate stride is a 'crossover' stride. It has extra

Javelin sequence.

length which allows the thrower to land in a 'lean back' position, once again extending the range over which the javelin can be thrown. This crossover stride lands the javelin thrower in the POWER position. A position common to all the throws and from which the thrower can 'strike'.

From this balanced position the throw begins with a drive of the back leg against a braced left side of the body and a straightening 'up and back' of the left leg. The right hip is driven vigorously forward by turning the right heal outwards. Finally, the javelin is lashed by the upper body and throwing arm, which has been left behind until the last moment. The throwing arm leads with the elbow which straightens, reaching as high as is possible. The throw is completed by the hand and the power is imparted to the javelin by a movement rather like waving it goodbye.

The Reverse

The whole movement is completed by a reverse step of the right leg which stops the thrower falling beyond the scratch line. Should the thrower step on or beyond this line the throw would be declared a 'no throw'. The thrower must walk back under control before leaving the throwing area.

Learning the Event
(for a right handed thrower)

With a soccer or basketball:

1   Practise a soccer style throw in, two feet together.

2   Practise a soccer style throw in, left foot forward.

The Schwanbeck exercise – practise this with a soccer or basketball.

3 Reach back to the side with the ball in both hands, twist the body forward, leaving the hands and ball back and from this position move to throw a soccer style throw in. This exercise is called a 'Schwanbeck'.

With a javelin and with a correct grip:

4 Stand as for a soccer style throw, take the non throwing hand away and throw at a target a few metres in front. A drinks can is ideal.

5 Throw from three strides beginning with the hand and arm back.

6 Throw from five strides. Start with the javelin above the shoulder. Walk the first two strides (the withdrawal strides) then accelerate into the final three throwing strides.

7 Practise the full throw from nine strides.

Special Safety

Javelins are very satisfying things to throw and considerable pleasure and educational value can be derived from the activity as long as no one behaves in a manner which is likely to give it a bad name. In the wrong hands they are no less dangerous now than they ever were! Therefore, great care and sensible behaviour must be demonstrated when learning and practising the event. Please read the chapter on safety very carefully where safety in throws is dealt with in some detail. In particular, it must be remembered javelins are relatively sharp at both ends. Consequently, no one should run to collect a javelin and you should always push it to the vertical before pulling it out of the ground.

THE SHOT PUTT

Explanation of the Event

Putting the weight, which is the traditional name of the event, has been passed down to modern athletics from traditional games such as the Scottish Highland Games. The implements used in the past were large stones, too heavy to be thrown, but suitable to be pushed one-handed from the shoulder. This natural action is now established as a rule, which ensures that the event continues unchanged in its format. In fact, the rule insists that the shot remains in close proximity to the chin until the delivery.

Principles of Shot Putting

The shot putt is a speed event. Although the weight of the shot itself suggests this is unlikely, the speed at which the thrower manages to deliver the shot is the main factor in deciding how far the shot travels. The other factors are angle of release and height of release. (See chapter on common elements of throwing). The problem for the shot putter is that this speed must be generated within the restricted area of the circle only 2.135 m across. The thrower's response to this problem is to try to increase the range over which the shot can be accelerated by muscle power. There are currently two ways of achieving this.

The Linear or O'Brien Technique The thrower faces the opposite direction to the throw and leans as far out of the back of the circle as is practicable. After accelerating across the circle and turning, the thrower pushes the shot with the hand as far in front of the stop board as possible, although the feet must remain within the circle.

The Rotational Technique The thrower mimics the discus technique and spins within the circle to accelerate himself and the shot which is tucked into the neck.

THE SHOT PUTT TECHNIQUE – LINEAR

Holding the Shot

No matter which of the two techniques is used the method of holding the shot is the same. It is held in the root of the fingers with the thumb and little finger spread a little either side to give it balance. There is some variation as to whether it is held under the chin or alongside the neck, depending on the athlete's ability to control it, but all shot coaches know the quote "that all shot putters should have a clean palm and a dirty neck!"

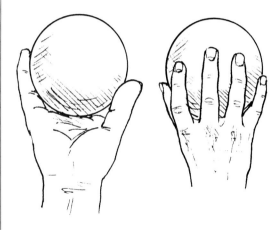

The shot putt grip.

The Glide

The thrower starts the throw facing the opposite direction to the throw. The body is bent forward and lowered with the non driving leg lifted behind, the whole body adopting a 'T' position. The rear leg is driven so that the thrower hops across the circle to land in the power position. The hop is kept as low as possible.

The Power Position to Delivery

The power position is a position common to the shot, discus and javelin and to some extent the hammer. It is the position in which the body is 'coiled' or primed and from which the thrower makes the actual throw. It is a balanced position and from it will come most of the force and consequently most of the distance of the throw.

The feet should be hip width apart so that the body can turn to the front without restriction and the shoulders should be square to the back. The chin, knee and toes should be in approximate vertical alignment from whichever angle the thrower is viewed.

From this position the throw is initiated by turning the right heel outwards, followed rapidly by an explosive straightening of the right leg. As the body is still facing backwards this creates torque in the trunk of the body. In a split second the left leg straightens back against the driving right leg and the body reacts to the torque applied and unwinds so that the thrower is facing the front. Finally, the arm straightens and the hand and fingers flip the shot away. The shot putter should be looking at the delivery hand as it completes the putt.

Shot putt sequence.

The Reverse

As a consequence of the explosive action of throwing the thrower may fall forward. To counter this and to save a 'no throw' the thrower should change feet and lower the centre of gravity – the reverse.

ROTATIONAL TECHNIQUE

The final delivery differs from that of the linear technique in that the final push of the shot is rather more of a sideways push because the body is rotating away from the direction of the throw. The rest of the technique so mimics the discus that you are referred to the chapter on discus throwing.

Learning the Event (for a right handed thrower)

With a soccer or basketball;

1   Practise a basketball push pass, two feet together.

2   Practise a basketball push pass, left foot forward. Step into the pass.

With a light shot or preferably a heavy bean bag:

3   Grip correctly, with feet together facing the front, bend knees – and throw.

4   As above, step back (imagine stepping on a spring) react – and throw.

5   As above, ensure the feet are correctly placed either side of a marked line.

6   Ensure each limb and body action is correct. Isolate and practise.

7   Use a shuffle, or step back as a preliminary shift. A side-on hop will suffice initially.

8   Practise a correct shift technique and gradually incorporate into the throw.

Special Safety

See chapter on safety relating to the throws.

THE HAMMER

Explanation of the Event

The hammer is a particularly spectacular event with a heavy metal ball attached to a wire handle travelling over 80 m at major events. Unfortunately, many people miss the occasion because it has to take place in safety, from within a cage and in the absence of surrounding track events. Having said that, in an attempt to stir up enthusiasm for the event a night-time meeting took place in London in the 1970's with sparklers attached to the hammer. Everything went well until one hammer and sparkler parted company!

The hammer as we know it was an Anglo/Irish activity, practised in such competitions as the Highland Games, although one would expect people to have thrown axes and hammers for as long as man has been able to attach stone or metal heads to wooden handles and in Scottish Highland Games the hammer handle is still made of wood not wire! The Irish took the sport to the U.S.A. and it was these Irish Americans that dominated the event in the early part of the 20th century.

Principles of Hammer Throwing

The thrower is restricted to a small circle and the only method of imparting the required momentum into the hammer is to spin around with the hammer at arm's length. The major factors governing the length of the throw are the speed of release (the thrower completes up to four turns to provide this) and the angle of release. The thrower provides the correct angle by starting the turns with the hammer rotating more or less around the horizontal axis and gradually steepening the angle before releasing it as near to the optimum angle of 45° as possible, although the hammer has no aerodynamic properties. The final ingredient, that of height of release, is of only minor significance in the hammer event and probably makes the optimum release angle somewhere between 42° and 44°. Speed is all-important and a ten per cent increase in the speed of the hammer head at release can improve a throw by up to 13 m. Hammer throwers seek the longest possible levers between themselves and the weight of the hammer and an increase of 3 cm in the length of the throwing lever can improve a throw by up to 3 m. Because of the forces involved, a 7.26 kg hammer can effectively feel as heavy as 320 kg to a world class thrower. A small head on the hammer also helps it travel further.

THE HAMMER THROW TECHNIQUE (for a right handed thrower)

Depending on the level of experience the thrower aims to complete between one and four turns.

The Grip

The handle is held in the left hand and the right hand is closed over it, as can be seen in the diagram.

The throw begins with the thrower facing the opposite way to the direction of the throw and standing at the back of the circle. The hammer head is placed just off the right foot. The hammer is usually swung twice around the head as preliminary swings to overcome inertia and to establish the correct path of travel. During these preliminary swings the hammer thrower gradually steepens the angle of the path of the hammer and establishes the low point of the swing to be in front of him or just off the right foot. As soon as the hammer arrives at the low point on the second preliminary swing the thrower begins to turn.

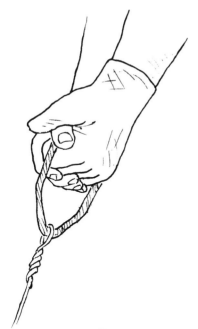

The hammer grip.

The Turns

The turns are made by initially rotating on the ball of the right foot and the heel of the left foot, together. The weight should be on the left foot. As the hammer reaches its high point the right foot is lifted from the ground and quickly moved around the left leg and placed back on the ground alongside the left leg. During this movement of the right leg the rest of the turn is completed on the sole of the left foot. The thrower should arrive back to the same position as at the start of the first turn. Subsequent turns should be of a similar format, each moving smoothly from one into the other. Gradually, throughout the turns the speed should be increased and the angle of the hammer steepened. The thrower will find it necessary to adopt a sitting position to counter the increasing force of the hammer, but the trunk should remain upright. During the turns the thrower

should allow the hammer to pull the arms out and stretch towards the hammer as it passes around the front, to increase the range of movement. The hammer should never be pulled in towards the thrower.

The Throw

As the final turn is completed, the thrower should have turned quickly enough so that the hammer is trailing him. From the high point of the hammer the thrower should sink downwards hauling the hammer down with him. As the hammer reaches its low point the thrower straightens up, driving with his legs and finally, with trunk and arms, delivers the hammer powerfully at the highest possible point.

Learning the Event

Using a football inside a polythene sack as an improvised hammer (for safety reasons):

1   Standing with feet hip width apart and an upright posture adopt a quarter sitting position. Point both arms towards the ground identifying the low point of the hammer swing. Maintaining that position take the left arm around and point upwards at the high point of the hammer swing.

2   Pick up the improvised hammer, grip with both hands and swing it around the head through the low and high points previously identified. Ensure the arms are fully extended when passing in front of the body.
    Place the hammer on the ground, off the right foot. Reach around and grip with the left hand. Grip with the right hand. Swing the hammer from that position up around and allow it to land in exactly the same position as at the start, back on the ground. Lift with the

legs from a bent knee and straight back position. Practise.

3 Start as number two. Make two swings around the head, the circles being as large as possible and release the improvised hammer over the left shoulder after the second turn. Ensure a good follow-through with the upper part of the body and arms.

4 Swinging the implement around the head, walk backwards and forwards for familiarity.

5 After two turns around the head try spinning with the hammer. Practise for familiarity. Identify a tree top in the distance. Use this as the high point of the hammer swing. Circle the hammer and walk around with it as it turns. Walk towards your focal point continually turning with the hammer. Focus the eyes on that high point on each pass as this ensures balance and stops giddiness.

6 Practise turning with the correct footwork.

Hammer sequence.

THROWING

7 From a cage using the correct grip with the correct hammer try a one turn throw.

8 Add further turns.

Special Safety

The hammer is a rotational event and consequently requires special care at all times and while it is unlikely, the hammer could slip out of the hand in any direction.

1 The event should be practised under non-slip conditions (ground and shoes).

2 Loose clothing is unsuitable.

3 When learning or teaching in groups more than adequate space must be allowed between the pupils.

4 Soft implements should be used until class control can be guaranteed.

5 Cages are provided at all proper stadiums and should be used for training and competition.

NOTE: Please see chapter on safety.

THE DISCUS

Explanation of the Event

The discus is thrown with a 'slinging' action and has always been a readily identifiable athletic event made famous by the statue from Ancient Greece, the 'Discobolus'. The sculptor was Myron. The discus was part of the ancient games but we do not know how heavy it was. When Robert Garrett picked up the discus at the first modern games in Athens in 1896 he was surprised to find how light it was compared with his home-made training discus. His was of solid iron, constructed by copying pictures of the ancient statue, but he still won! However, the discus is not light; it is too heavy to throw like a javelin and the implement thrown by adult men weighs 2 kg.

Principles of Discus Throwing

The discus thrower is confined to the circle, 2.5 m in diameter, and must project the discus as far as possible. The distance the discus travels depends on the speed, height and angle at which it is released. The confinement within the circle and the weight of the discus oblige the thrower to rotate to generate the required force. By whirling around, the discus thrower can gradually increase the speed of the discus and the modern technique of 1½ turns means the discus travels as far as 9 m from start to release during its acceleration.

But this is only the beginning, for the discus is an aerodynamic implement. In principle, its shape is similar to an aircraft's wing and while it will not fly as easily as a 'frisbee', thrown correctly it gives the expert a considerable advantage. Throwing the

The discus throwing technique demands all-round body strength building to a crescendo of power and timing at the point of release.

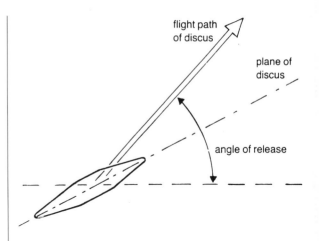

discus correctly means a number of things. It should be thown at an angle somewhere between 30° and 40°. (Not 45°, which is the optimum angle for a projectile.) The nose should be kept down slightly. The discus should not be in line with the flightpath but at a rather flatter angle. The discus must spin to keep its position of flight correct. Once the spinning slows, the near edge of the discus will drop. This means that instead of the sharp edge of the discus cutting through the air, the flat face will produce more resistance and the discuss will fall from the sky. In other words, the discuss will stall, exactly as an aircraft will if the tail drops.

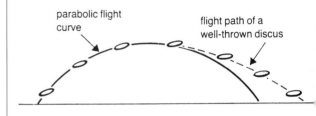

Normal flight curve of a well thrown, aerodynamic discus.

Aircraft always take off into the wind. This is because it is the aircraft's speed in relation to the air that is important to create lift, not its speed in relation to the ground. It is the same with the discus. An oncoming breeze to the thrower's arm gives the discus that extra lift and consequently discus circles are often sited to make the best of the local prevailing winds. The discus throw therefore, is very much a thoughtful person's event!

THE DISCUS TECHNIQUE

The Grip

The discus is held in the favourite hand and gripped rather as one would hold a suitcase. It is held lightly in the fingertips, at arm's length. The hand is the only contact with the discus and the part of the body that transfers all the force into the discus. Consequently, it is essential that the grip is absolutely correct. Some throwers like to keep their first two fingers close together for extra purchase.

The Turn
(for a right handed thrower)

IT IS VITAL THAT THE THROW IS COMPLETED IN AN EASY, RELAXED AND BALANCED MANNER, even though enormous forces are in play.

The accomplished thrower throws with 1½ turns, although by the time a preliminary 'wind up' has been added the upper half of the body completes almost 2 turns. The throw begins with the thrower facing opposite to the direction of the throw. The feet should be slightly wider than hip width apart. One or two easy preliminary swings are performed with the thrower transferring his body weight naturally from foot to foot.

On completion of these swings the thrower enters the turn, turning left with the body weight over the left foot. A half sitting position is adopted. The trunk and head should be upright.

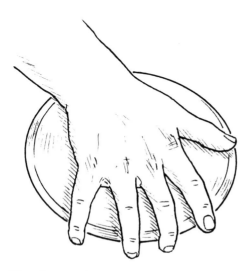

The discus grip.

Preliminary swings.

THROWING

The head is very much the rudder as the thrower spins, and a good idea is for the thrower to pick out a focal spot on the horizon at about 10 o'clock. The arms are extended in balance, the throwing (right) arm carried just behind the right hip and the turn should be started without undue haste. The body should turn as a whole and in complete synchronisation with itself. The discus is a very balletic event. Once the thrower is facing the front he almost runs across the circle, driving from the left leg. The right foot steps down onto the centre of the circle. It is essential that the right foot keeps turning once it is grounded. The right leg remains bent as in the half sitting position already mentioned. The discus arm is deliberately positioned at a high point up towards the focal point at 10 o'clock. The discus is now well behind the thrower and he will be wound up rather like a spring waiting to be released.

The athlete should arrive in this THROWING POSITION on balance, which should mean that the chin, right knee and right toe are in vertical alignment. The front, or left, foot must be grounded quickly because the throw cannot effectively begin until this has been done. This foot must also land in such a position that the feet are hip width apart when the thrower finally turns to face the direction of the throw. If the feet are too much in line the hips will be blocked. Too wide apart and the left leg cannot provide the brace for the throw. From the 'throwing position' the right heel is turned outwards increasing the torque, or 'wound up' position even more. This also drives the right hip forward. Initially, the discus is swung downwards through the greatest range possible and using gravity to its greatest effect, before the throwing arc continues it upward on its 'take-off' path. The whole body is uncoiled and the

Entering the turn.

Winding up.

right leg drives explosively forward and upward through the hips and chest, indeed discus coaches say the hips throw the discus. Finally, the throwing arm, which has been left well behind, hurls the discus with a whip-like action. It is possible to bring the non-throwing arm close into the body during the final stages to increase the rotational range of the throwing arm, but this should not be done at the expense of a good right side drive.

Throwers vary in their style of final release. Some, especially women, throw from a fixed feet position. Others continue the turn after the throw has been made and reverse their feet to avoid falling out of the front of the circle. Either is acceptable. The sequence shows an active reverse, not a fixed feet throw.

Learning the Event

With a quoit or a heavy bean bag (½ kg):

1   Stand with feet hip width apart. Hold the implement in the favourite hand and extend arms sideways to the horizontal. Practise turning the body allowing the arms to swing with the body backwards and forwards.

2   On the second swing forwards throw the implement in the direction the feet are facing. Allow the knees to bend as the arm and body rotate backwards and encourage the legs to straighten as the discus is swung forward.

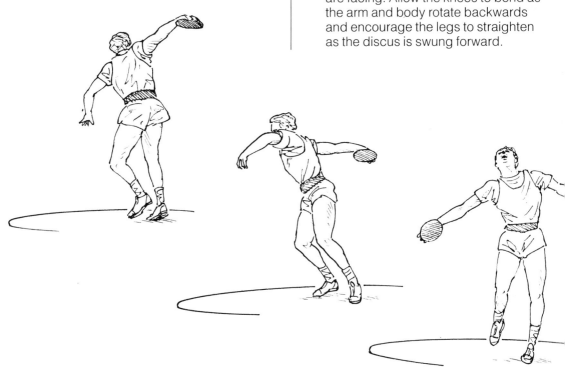

Arriving in the throwing position.   *The throw.*

3 As above, but on the second swing backwards step back with the right foot and throw. Encourage the back foot to push the right hip forward as the throw is initiated. (Standing throw).

4 Introduce one turn. Stand facing the direction of the throw with feet hip width apart. Swing the arms and body backwards. As they swing forward run forward with the right foot. Rotate on the right foot as it lands and take the left foot to the front of the circle. This stepping and turning action should bring the thrower to a similar position as when throwing from a standing row.

With the correct discus and using the correct grip:

5 Practise 1 to 4.

6 Learn the complete throwing action.

Special Safety

The discus is a rotational event and consequently requires special care at all times and while it is unlikely, the discus could slip out of the hand in any direction.

1 The event should be practised under non slip conditions – ground and shoes.

2 Loose clothing is unsuitable.

3 When learning or teaching in groups more than adequate space must be allowed between the pupils.

4 Soft implements should be used until class control can be guaranteed.

5 Cages are provided at all proper stadiums and should be used for training and competition.

NOTE: Please see chapter on safety.

COMBINED EVENTS – DECATHLON, HEPTATHLON

EXPLANATION

The decathlon for men and the heptathlon for women are competitions to find out who is the best all-round athlete. The individual events in each are as follows:

Decathlon

Day 1. 100 m, Long Jump, Shot Putt, High Jump, 400 m.
Day 2. 100 m Hurdles, Discus, Pole Vault, Javelin, 1500 m.

Heptathlon

Day 1. 100 m Hurdles, High Jump, Shot Putt, 200 m.
Day 2. Long Jump, Javelin, 800 m.

These events must be competed in the order listed above and if practicable there should be at least a thirty minute break between events.

Combined Events competitions are different to all other events in athletics in that the winner is the one who can score the most points. Scoring tables have been produced by the International Athletic Federation in which each event has been allocated points relative to the time, distance or height achieved. It does not matter who wins the most individual competitions. What does matter is who has scored the most points according to the tables at the end of the two days. In the 1960 Olympic Games decathlon competition Yang Chuang Kwang of Formosa won eight of the ten events and yet only gained the silver medal. Rafer Johnson managed to score only marginally less than Kwang in those eight events but out-scored him easily in the other two events. The concept of finding the best 'all-rounder' is a natural one that is not confined to athletics. Water sports, Nordic sports (skiing etc.) and even team games such as cricket have competitions to find the best 'all-rounder'. The Greeks in their classical Olympic Games had such a competition called the Pentathlon. The events were the long jump, discus, javelin, 192 m sprint and wrestling.

The men's event has remained stable for many years although in 1912 at the Stockholm Olympic Games it took three days to complete the decathlon. The women's event was only introduced to the Olympic Games in 1964 as a pentathlon and became the heptathlon in 1984. There is pressure, albeit slight at the moment, to change to the decathlon in the future.

Rules of Competition

Each individual event in athletics has its own set of rules. These rules apply to the events of the Combined Event competition. There are however, one or two occasions when this event has its own, quite separate rule. For example, in the long jump and in the throwing events, each competitor is allowed three trials only, and in the running events and hurdles a competitor is disqualified from any event in which he has made three, not two, false starts.

Principles of Combined Events

Once an athlete can perform each of the events to a reasonable level, the combined event competition is one of understanding the points system in relation to the way the human body works. A study of the ten men's events shows us the following:

1   Only the 1500 m requires the athlete to have aerobic endurance.

2   Only the 1500 m encourages the athlete to be light in physique.

3   All the other nine events require the athlete to use very high speeds of movement.

4   Five of the events, 100 m, 400 m, long jump, pole vault and 110m hurdles require the athlete to be a fast runner.

5   The javelin, the pole vault and the hurdles require high levels of skill.

6   A large physique would benefit the three throws but would be detrimental to all the other events especially the 1500 m.

This mass of interesting information suggests that a variety of different types of athletes could be successful at combined events. Daley Thompson of Great Britain (height 1.85 m, weight 88 kg, age 30) and Jurgen Hingsen of Germany (height 2.00 m, weight 102 kg, age 30) were arch rivals but show considerable differences in their respective physiques. However, they both possessed the common factors of skill, speed and power.

In the women's heptathlon the following should be noted:

1   Running speed is very important for the 200 m, long jump and 100 m hurdles.

2   All the events, except the 800 m require the athlete to be able to move at high speed.

3   Anaerobic fitness is essential for the 200 m and the 800 m.

4   The javelin and the hurdles require high levels of skill.

5   A large physique would be beneficial for the shot.

Therefore it makes sense for the athlete to concentrate on training that helps her to run fast, jump and hurdle. Javelin has very special considerations but excellent results can be achieved with a similar sized physique as the jumper/hurdler and so the shot putt, while practised frequently, has to be achieved at the expense of a shot putter's massive body weight.

One of the major problems for a combined events athlete is that there are so many events that need to be practised and so much conditioning that needs to accompany this practise that there is not enough time available, nor enough energy, to accomplish everything that needs to be done. Therefore, success at combined events depends very much on the personal organisation the athlete brings to preparation. The intelligent athlete will look for common elements in their training. For example, sprint training will help the 100 m, the 400 m, the long jump, the pole vault and the 110 m hurdles. There are three jumps, the pole vault, the long jump and the high jump. There are three throws, the javelin, the discus and the shot. The athlete would be wise to compartmentalise his training to make maximum use of his time and balance that against the time each specialist event requires. In earlier chapters the similarities between events has been highlighted.

TECHNIQUE (COMPETITION)

The combined events competition lasts two days, sometimes starting as early as 9.30 am in the morning and not finishing until late in the evening. Imagine how the decathlete feels trying to warm up for the 110 m hurdles on the second day at 8.30 am in the morning after the previous day's exertions which finished with the 400 m! Actually, the combined event athlete only competes flat out for about seven to ten minutes in those two days. However, reserves of energy are devastated because those efforts are so concentrated

The women's heptathlon and men's decathlon offers all-rounders the chance of success where their ability in individual disciples would not.

and because the athlete is constantly warming up, warming down, rehearsing and riding a roller-coaster of emotion. While success is to the fore everything is fine, but at some stage during the competition things will inevitably go badly. The athlete cannot afford to dwell on what is past but must concentate positively on what is about to happen. A brief insight into what is likely is therefore worthwhile.

Athletes should arrive at the track in time to establish themselves, warm up, be well rehearsed mentally and physically and give themselves ten to fifteen minutes for detailed items of organisation, such as 'checking in' and putting numbers on vests – on both days. The initial warm-up should suffice for the day except for a few light stride runs between events and special practices required for the technical events. Mental concentration is required for each event and while that may be quite simple initially, it is easy to succumb to a lapse during drawn out events such as the high jump. The discus presents special problems for the men in that all the events that precede it demand linear power. The discus requires balletic balance and rhythm and the athlete must adapt or pay the likely unfortunate consequences!

An athlete cannot compete on air alone. Food and especially drink must be taken at regular intervals. This requires considerable thought and organisation so that it enhances performance rather than detracts from it. Drink, especially isotonic ones that replenish the minerals lost by sweating, should be sipped regularly especially early in the day, such as after the 100 m or 110 m hurdles, since dehydration is the athlete's main enemy. High energy foods that are easily digested should be taken at suitable times. These are personal but some such opportunities may be, in the decathlon, immediately after the shot and after the pole vault warm-up, unless the athlete is first to vault, and in the heptathlon, after the high jump, unless the

athlete is among the best and therefore last to jump, in which case immediately after the high jump warm-up is more suitable. On the second day, after the long jump might suit the athlete.

Athletes only have three attempts in the throwing and jumping events unlike many individual event competitions where six attempts is the norm. A zero score resulting from three no jumps will not result in disqualification, for the athlete can only be disqualified for not making an attempt, but to score no points would be disastrous for the final outcome. Therefore, the beginner would be advised to be conservative and ensure a 'safe' approach to the first competitions they attempt. The following basics are advised:

100 m	block start – signs of good running technique – run right through the finish.
200/400 m	block start – controlled pace.
800/1500 m	signs of pace control.
100/110 hurdles	block start – correct hurdle action – 3 stride pattern.
Long jump	standing start to run-up – measured 14 stride approach – correct take-off action.
Pole vault	standing start to run-up – measured 10/14 stride approach – correct plant/take-off action – swing – simple turn and pole pushed away.
High jump	standing start to run-up – measured 6/8 stride approach, 3 on final curve – correct take-off action – flop.

Shot	2 throws from power position – final throw with shift.
Javelin	standing start to run-up – one throw from 5 strides – high arm action – final throw from full 4–2–3 run-up.
Discus	2 throws from power position – final throw from one turn.

Finally, the combined event athlete must be prepared for all eventualities and therefore a large bag which might include the following is advised.

A Checklist of Essential Items Required by the Combined Event Athlete

Clothing

Vests	– four
Shorts	– four
Socks	– four pairs – two per day
Sweat shirts and sweaters	– cooling is a constant problem
Tracksuits	– two if possible
Waterproof tracksuit	– one
Spikes	– two pairs preferably
Training shoes	– two pairs preferably
Specialist event shoes	– high jump shoes, javelin boots, etc. (if available)
Towels	– three at least
Hat	– for sun and rain
Sleeping bag, quilted suit or blanket	– to provide warmth

Hardware

Extra screw-in spikes	– variety of sizes (some tracks have a 6mm limit)
Spike spanner	– to change spikes
Pincers	– for the one screw-in spike that will not come out!
Old towel	– for wiping throwing implements
Resin	– for pole vault and javelin grips
Tape	– for pole vault grip
Spare pole tips	– for vaulting poles
Measuring tape	– to measure run-ups
Spiked marker	– for pole vault and long jump run-up
Talcum powder or tape	– for high jump run-up
First Aid	– Elastoplast, antiseptic cream
Large drink containers	– for sun or rain.

Alternative Combined Events

Combined Events competitions are not confined to those already mentioned. For example, many countries modify the programme to give juniors an opportunity to experience combined events, for example in Great Britain an octathlon is held, and the I.A.A.F. recognises a men's pentathlon. Indoor competitions are sometimes held as a men's octathlon and a women's pentathlon. The 'Blitz' decathlon is occasionally attempted in which all events must be completed within an hour, however, this is not an official IAAF event.

NOTE: I.A.A.F. Combined Event Tables can be bought from the British Athletic Federation Bookshop. (See chapter on 'Useful Addresses')

SAFETY AND TRAINING

SAFETY IN ATHLETICS

Athletics is not generally regarded as a hazardous activity, especially when compared to the dangers of motor racing or collision sports such as rugby or American football. However, it is essential to be aware of what can go wrong and how such accidents can be avoided. Good organisation and individual consideration should prevent all accidents but there are two areas of possible danger, collisions and falls. Collisions with other people, or worse with flying implements such as javelins and hammers and falls, especially in the pole vault, high jump and steeplechase. All collisions can be avoided on the track by following a simple etiquette. Every club and changing room should have a straightforward code of conduct listed on the notice board, which should include rules for safe and courteous behaviour at all points of the track.

Safety in Throws

Accidents in throwing are unacceptable and avoidable if the following rules are adhered to.

Only those adults who are qualified coaches or physical education teachers should undertake to look after groups of young people learning to throw. Their qualification should ensure they are insured.

Only equipment and facilities suitable for the age and stage of the athlete should be used.

All throwing sessions must take place in strictly controlled situations. Non-throwers should wait for their turn by standing well behind the thrower. Everyone must concentrate. There must be no foolish behaviour and nothing must distract the thrower.

NEVER throw when anyone is in front of you.

NEVER stand in front of anyone who is throwing.

NEVER wear loose, flappy clothing.

ONLY throw in designated areas.

ONLY throw in one, designated direction.

ALWAYS walk to retrieve the implements.

ALWAYS carry javelins point down.

ALWAYS wear appropriate footwear so that you do not slip.

BEWARE, especially when it is wet and slippery.

Throwers are more likely to injure others if equipment is faulty. Throwing cages should be inspected for gaps and secure fixings. Hammers, in particular, need regular checks, indeed the hammer must have very special considerations and should be thrown from a cage designed for that purpose.

Safety in the Jumps

It is unwise to train alone, especially in the pole vault and high jump, just in case something does go wrong. So do ensure that there is always someone on hand.

It is very important to use facilities appropriate to the age and ability level of the athlete.

ALWAYS look before crossing the run-up or run-up area, just as you would when crossing the road.

Athletes must take responsibility for their own welfare, not least by checking their equipment themselves. Track surfaces should be suitable, not slippery or worn enough to cause accidents. Landing areas should be suitable for the activities being attempted. There should be no gaps between the mats, check that they are not hidden by the cover. Sand pits may contain hidden dangers; nails, stones, tins and bottles have all been discovered in jumping pits. Unfortunately, vandalism and dogs cannot be ignored, consequently, all sand pits should be checked and dug before use. Surrounding areas of landing areas, pits, steeplechase barriers and finishing lines should all be clear of rakes, hurdles, hurdle weights, tables, chairs and similar paraphernalia. If hurdles are to be used in the session they should be checked to ensure the tops are smooth and that the weights are secure.

These notes are written as a guide and are not intended to be a comprehensive document. Official instructions on the safety of track and field can be obtained from the British Athletic Federation and from The English Schools Athletic Association whose addresses appear at the end of the book.

Internal Injuries

These are frequently self inflicted. Tears and pulls of muscles, tendons and ligaments, and other medical problems, can be caused by self-abuse often brought about by lack of knowledge. Certain considerations are therefore essential.

Warm-up

It is said that performance can be improved by up to 15 per cent simply by raising the internal temperature of the body by one degree, although obviously, there is an upper limit here. The warm-up should be a series of exercises that progress the athlete from their state of normal living to the readiness for explosive movement. It should include exercises such as jogging, to raise the body temperature, stretching exercises, to warn the body of the impending range of movement expected, specific skill practices and finally competition type exercises to complete the preparation.

Warm-down

After exercise it is also important to return the body back to normal living in a progressive manner. Light running encourages blood circulation which removes waste products such as lactic acid, massages the muscles and takes nutrients to tired parts for immediate repair. However, the warm-down is not an endurance session.

Warm-ups and warm-downs should be very personal because one man's warm up may be another man's work-out! It also helps enormously if the activities are enjoyable.

Shoes

Many injuries are caused by incorrect footware. Worn heels can cause all sorts of problems, over-large heel tabs dig into the achilles tendon and modern sales gimmicks do not suit all feet. The potential athlete should choose athletic footware carefully and to wear them in gradually.

Clothing

It is most important that the athlete is warm and able to concentrate on the training, consequently clothes should be of suitable material and sensibly tailored.

Training surfaces

Running on the camber of a road can often produce injuries, not just to the feet and ankles but to knees, hips, back and muscles of the legs and lower trunk. It is surprising how many supposed injuries to the legs have their origin in the lower back! Running on a natural surface, such as level grass certainly limits injuries, however, restricting one's training to a single surface can bring on shin splints when a change is inevitable, that is to say if a road runner moves to grass muscle soreness might result just as much as if a grass runner moves to the track!

Drugs

Throughout the history of sport competitors have sought to gain an advantage over their opponents by taking performance-enhancing substances – drugs. The ancient Greeks ate sheep's testicles and strychnine was used during the nineteenth century! Modern technology has produced many substances suitable for medicine but which may be used to improve sporting performances. However, THE TAKING OF DRUGS FOR ANY REASON OTHER THAN MEDICAL IS DANGEROUS AND AGAINST ALL THE RULES AND ETHICS OF SPORT. Recently, more and more evidence has emerged on the damage caused by drugs such as anabolic steroids, growth hormones and amphetamines. Sportsmen are known to have died as a result of abusing these substances.

The British Athletic Federation was the first sports governing body to implement a random drug testing scheme, voting it into place in 1986. All athletes should understand what may be involved when invited to take a 'drugs test'. They should also appreciate that it is for their own benefit, to protect them against cheats.

One problem caused by the legislation is that athletes who are unwell may take banned substances by mistake. Flu or cold remedies may contain Pseudo Ephidrene whilst others may contain Codeine. Both are on the unacceptable list. You would be wise to contact the National Athletics Federation or Sports Council and ask for a list of banned substances to ensure you do not contravene the rules accidentally. You would also be advised to consult your doctor.

Complete information on the subject of banned drugs and acceptable alternatives are produced by the British Athletic Federation and The Sports Council. Addresses are in the chapter 'Useful Addresses.'

TRAINING TO IMPROVE PERFORMANCE AND TO PREVENT INJURY

Training is essential to improve performance. Or is it? Injuries are certainly caused because of a lack of the proper preparation. This may range from no training to inappropriate training or even too much training. There are certain concepts that must be understood to get the best performance from training and to avoid injury.

The hammer throw is a unique athletic discipline requiring special strengths and abilities.

Training makes you worse! Ask anyone that has just undertaken a severe strength or endurance session. They feel exhausted and could have performed better at the beginning than at the end of the session. Therefore,

TRAINING + REST = IMPROVEMENT.

The rest required after each session varies from activity to activity and from athlete to athlete. High intensity sessions such as hopping and bounding or flat out throwing require longer recoveries than less dynamic sessions such as conditioning circuit training sessions. Qualified coaches are trained to know and understand this very complicated subject so an ambitious athlete is advised to request help at an early stage, before mistakes are made.

Training Programmes

A training programme is one that must be constructed just as a building is, with foundations, supporting structures and a roof, before the flag of high performance can be flown from the top!

An ABC of Training

A is for accuracy

The overall plan should be accurate in its method and detail. The exercises set should be accurate in relation to the ambition and age of the athlete and they should also be accurate in their intensity and amount.

B is for balance

The athlete's lifestyle should be balanced between work, sport and leisure. The training programme should be balanced between work and rest. Exercises should be balanced so that the body remains in balance, for example, the trunk must be as

strong as the limbs, the back must be as strong as the front, the top must be as strong as the bottom, otherwise injury will inevitably occur.

C is for continuity

The development of athletic performance is a process. An athlete that manages to train successfully for a whole winter will have a distinct advantage over those that start and stop. Likewise, an athlete that continues to work and compete over a number of years without breaks, other than those that are planned, is much more likely to be successful than one that follows a haphazard and inconsistent programme.

The Five 'S's

When planning a training and competition programme the beginner would be wise to keep things simple, but the training programme should definitely include all of the following elements to a certain degree.

Suppleness

An overall stretching programme should be completed regularly. Top athletes complete stretching exercises almost every day. These exercises should be done steadily and without pain to improve the range of movement and to avoid injury. Stretching should be done after the initial part of the warm-up and before any other activity. A few more stretching exercises should also be done after the session has finished.

Skill

All field events require infinite levels of skill and these should be practised immediately after the warm-up while the athlete is fresh and receptive to learning, otherwise it will be less effective and may even result in injury. Only very experienced athletes should practise their skill when tired.

Speed

Speed is ultimately the limiting factor to performance. All the best athletes are very fast, not necessarily in their running, although it is essential to all the jumps, but in their body movements; world class javelin throwers release the javelin at over 80 miles per hour! This is the fastest human movement in athletics; the only movement that is faster is the speed of the hammer-head as the athlete releases it. Speed is skill performed quickly and therefore the same rule applies: the athlete must be fresh. So speed should be practised after skill but before tiring conditioning work.

Strength

There are many ways of training for strength. Throwers, jumpers and combined events athletes require power, which is strength × speed, it is no good if the athlete is very strong but slow. There are special methods of training for power which are beyond the covers of this book, however, strength training is, by definition, a very tiring process. Therefore, it should be undertaken after mobility, skill and speed training.

Stamina

Throwers and jumpers take very little time to complete their exercise in competition. A shot putter takes no more than two to three seconds to complete one putt and a pole vaulter no more than ten seconds to complete the vault. Nevertheless, both athletes require stamina of some sort, even if it is only to help them train for longer periods of time. Any endurance training must take place last.

Children cannot work particularly hard because they simply do not possess the capacity to do so. Their bodies are too small, so as long as one does not overwork them it does not matter too much what activity they undertake from day to day.

Teenagers and adults, on the other hand, take quite long periods of time to recover from the much harder sessions they are able to undertake. It can take 48 hours to recover from a strength session during which time the body is rebuilding. It does not make sense to sprint flat out while the body is not at its best, it can lead to injury. To avoid this problem an athlete might practise the following programme.

Day one   – skill and speed
Day two   – strength
Day three – endurance
Day four   – rest

Repeating the sequence on days, 5, 6, 7 and 8.

An athlete would be wise to include a light training week every fourth week. This may mean cutting the amount of work (not the quality of the work) by fifty per cent, or in the case of some international athletes, seventy-five per cent. Once again, this can be a complicated business but qualified coaches are trained to be able to give athletes personal advice.

Note: Adults (over the age of 18) who wish to become qualified should contact the British Athletic Federation, or the I.A.A.F. for information. In Great Britain and Northern Ireland there will be courses in your area.

RULES CLINIC

How can I discover exactly what the rules are?

It is very important that competitors know the rules of their competition thoroughly. The rules are there to ensure each athlete knows exactly what to expect and ensures they have a fair chance. Those athletes that do not know the rules put themselves at a disadvantage. The International Amateur Athletic Federation Handbook contains all the rules for international competition. However, it is not unusual for countries or area associations to have their own version of the rules for domestic competition and it is important to have a copy of them as well. A handbook called 'Rules for Competition' contains the official variation of the rules for the British Athletic Federation. The rules are occasionally changed if they become outdated or inappropriate and it is important to possess an up-to-date version.

It is a simple matter to buy a copy of the rules. They may be on sale at athletic bookshops at major competitions or they can be bought from the relevant association. Please see the chapter of 'Useful Addresses'.

What must I wear?

You must wear a vest and a pair of shorts and they must remain 'decent' if they get wet! You are advised to wear a pair of shoes suitable for the competition. In the Shot, Discus and Hammer smooth soles are more suitable for the concrete circle but in the Javelin and all the Jumps spiked shoes help you to grip, especially in wet weather. There are strict rules governing the length and number of spikes shoes are allowed and each running track may have a set of 'house rules' insisting that spikes be restricted to a particular size so that they will not damage the track.

How many attempts do I get?

In the jumps you are allowed three attempts at each height until you have recorded three consecutive failures. You do not have to attempt every height.

In the throws you are allowed three to six throws depending on the decision of the meeting organiser. It is essential you check how many attempts you will be allowed before the competition begins. Sometimes, when there are a large number of competitors everyone will be allowed three throws but only the top six or eight competitors will be allowed three further throws.

Combined event rules are different. Please see under the combined event chapter.

How do I win?

By throwing the furthest or by jumping the highest. In the event of a tie, which is highly unlikely in the javelin but not infrequent in the high jump, the result is referred. In the throws and horizontal jumps the person who has the second-best effort is declared the winner. In the vertical jumps the person who cleared on the first attempt is placed in front of anyone who cleared the same height on the second attempt.

Who goes first?

A draw will be made by the organisers and you will be told the competition order before the start. You are advised to listen carefully and check the order, especially the names of the competitors just before you, so that you can get ready in plenty of time for your turn when it comes around. If you are in more than one event at the same time you should report to the judges in charge of the events and explain your predicament. It is possible to change the field event order but it is not possible to hold up a track race; track takes priority.

Must I wear a number?

If the organisers provide them, yes you must. Every athlete must wear two numbers, one on their chest and one on their back except the pole vaulters and high jumpers who need only wear one. You would be wise to include eight safety pins in your kit-bag so that you can pin your numbers to your vest.

Can I use my own equipment or must I use those provided?

In most competitions you are allowed to use your own javelin or other throwing implement. Be careful, it must be checked by the organisers well before the competition starts to ensure it conforms to the rules, and therefore you must arrive in plenty of time and find out where it is to be checked. Once you have handed it in you are unlikely to be given it back before the competition starts. You must also be prepared to allow everyone else in the competition to use it, but pole vaulters who possess their own vaulting poles do not have to share them with other competitors due to their individual nature.

Can I wait for the wind to blow the right way to help me?

Yes you can, but you are not allowed to keep everyone waiting for an unreasonable amount of time. In fact, each trial should be completed within one and a half minutes, although once again pole vaulters have a dispensation and are allowed two minutes. This is another reason why you should know the order of competition and be ready to compete, so as not to waste your own valuable time.

Combined event rules are different. Please see under the combined event chapter.

Are the lines in or out?

Out! If you or the implement touch one of the scratch or sector lines the attempt is considered invalid. In the high jump the plane of the uprights and crossbar are considered the line and in the pole vault it is the plane of the back of the box.

Am I allowed to put marks down so that I am sure my run-up will be correct?

Yes you can, but it is not normal for you to be allowed to mark the run-up itself. It is best to put a marker along side the runway, something that cannot be accidentally kicked away. High jumpers should use sticky tape. If in doubt, check with the officials looking after your competition.

Can my coach help me during the competition?

You would be wise to have a coach who can help you organise yourself before the competition starts but it is your competition and you should attempt to be self sufficient. Once the competition begins you are not allowed to communicate with your coach.

What if the equipment breaks – vaulting pole, javelin, hammer etc.

It is important that the competition is conducted fairly. Therefore, if the equipment breaks you are not penalised and are allowed that attempt again.

Do I have to take a drug test if I am asked?

Yes! But you do not have to take it until all your events are completed, that day.

You are advised to ensure you are accompanied by your team manager or other suitable person.

EQUIPMENT

Training Shoes

All athletes need a flat soled pair of shoes for the vast majority of their training time. Almost all training will be done in these shoes, except for actual competition practises. It is important that these shoes are chosen with care. Fashions do not always suit individual feet and the athlete must be strong-willed enough to put fashion behind effective use. The athlete should look for comfortable shoes that:

1   Give the feet adequate support.

2   Have a raised heel as in normal shoes.

3   Have a reasonably wide heel base, so as not to twist the ankle.

4   Do not dig into the achilles tendon because the heel tabs are too high.

5   Are relatively light.

6   Do not slip.

7   Do not leave marks on gymnasium floors.

Basketball boots are unacceptable, but there are many good shoes on the market at a variety of prices.

The athlete is about to unleash a sequence of movements that will see the shot released at the highest possible point.

Competition Shoes

Once the athlete has passed the introductory stage, a pair of competition shoes becomes important. Initially, most jumpers find a simple pair of spiked shoes adequate provided that they have a reasonably raised heel. Shoes should have built up heels because no heels on the shoes can result in painful stretching of the achilles tendons. Sprint spikes often have no heels because of the nature of that event, avoid these and look for middle distance spikes or general purpose spiked shoes. When choosing a pair of spikes for jumping check that the sole is strong throughout the length of the sole. A highly flexible shoe will not give the take-off foot adequate support. The shoes should have soles for screw-in spikes and high jumpers will need shoes that have heel spikes, as will javelin throwers. Initially, for junior javelin throwers relatively light shoes are adequate but more senior throwers will need strong supportive shoes or even boots. These can be bought, at a price, from specialist shops and are frequently advertised in athletic magazines. However, if training is practised on a grass field, which is quite acceptable, a pair of football boots is a sensible option. They give plenty of support and have the necessary heel studs to stop slipping, however they will not be allowed on plastic surfaces.

Simple, flat soled shoes are best for the discus, shot and hammer. Normal training shoes have broad heels and a tread on the sole which restricts smooth turns or glides. Old-fashioned gym shoes are as good as anything but expensive shoes are available from athletic shoe companies.

Tracksuit

Warmth is essential to the would-be athlete. It aids performance and helps avoid injury. It is the first priority and any clothes that keep the athlete warm will do, as long as they are not dangerous by being too tight or too loose. Old trousers, slacks or jeans and warm jumpers will suffice until the athlete is committed. Eventually, a tracksuit will become almost inevitable and the athlete should look carefully to check it fits the necessary requirements, which are:

1   It keeps you warm.

2   It is wind-proof.

3   It is easy to remove without catching in spiked shoes and should have long zips for this purpose. (Remember, field event athletes spend their athletic careers taking off and putting on tracksuits to keep warm between attempts or training efforts!). Because of the treatment field event athletes inevitably give their clothes, the suit must be sturdy.

4   It is easily washable.

5   It should look good! Confidence is everything in athletics and the athlete must feel good about himself.

6   It is comfortable.
A shower-proof suit will eventually become a must and if the tracksuit can do both jobs so be it. However, it is important to choose a suit that breathes and does not leave the athlete wetter inside, because of condensation, than outside.

High jump and pole vault competitions take a long time and the athletes are exposed to the elements for long periods. A good umbrella is a worthwhile investment for protection against sun and rain.

The serious combined events athlete requires a wardrobe of equipment, and all athletes would be advised to study the list included in that chapter.

Implements (Javelins, Poles, etc.)

It is beyond the scope of this book to advise on personal athletic equipment. Expert advice should be taken before spending good money and the athletic club is the best place to go for it. Athletes need their own equipment for training and it can be acquired from specialist athletic shops. Once again, if there is any difficulty in finding a shop, or advice, your national association can help.

USEFUL ADDRESSES

BRITISH ATHLETIC FEDERATION (B.A.F.)
225A Bristol Road
Edgbaston
Birmingham
B5 7UB.
Tel: 021 440 5000

Note: The B.A.F. organises the coaching of athletics in Great Britain and Northern Ireland and the education of people wishing to become coaches through its National Coaches. There are eleven spread throughout the country and one is responsible for your area. Their names, addresses and telephone numbers are available from the B.A.F.

BAF Athletics Bookcentre
5 Church Road
Bookham
Surrey
KT23 3PN.
Tel: 0372 452804

WORLD GOVERNING BODY
International Amateur Athletic Federation (I.A.A.F.)
3 Hans Crescent
Knightsbridge
London
SW1X 0LN.
Tel: 071 581 8771

British Olympic Association
1 Wandsworth Plain
London
SW18 1ET.
Tel: 081 871 2677

The Sports Council – England
16 Upper Woburn Place
London
WC1H 0QW.
Tel: 071 388 1277

Sports Aid Foundation
16 Upper Woburn Place
London
WC1H 0QW.
Tel: 071 387 9380

English Schools Athletic Association
26 Newborough Green
New Malden
Surrey
KT3 5HS.
Tel: 081 949 1506

Scottish Schools Athletic Association
11 Muirfield Street
Kirkcaldy
Fife
KY2 6SY.
Tel: 0592 260168

Ulster Schools Athletic Association
c/o Belfast Royal Academy
Cliftonville Road
Belfast
BT14 6JL.

Welsh Schools Athletic Association
Neuadd Wen
Trefeglwys Road
Llanidloes
Powys
SY18 6JA.
Tel: 05512 2156

British Athletics Supporters Club
11 Railway Road
Newbury
Berks
RG14 7PE.
Tel: 0635 33400

National Union of Track Statisticians
2 Chudleigh Close
Bedford
MK40 3AW.
Tel: 0234 344407

Novice high jumpers can only progress when a safe landing is ensured.

INDEX

RULES CLINIC
INDEX